HITLER'S SPANISH DIVISION

DEDICATION

To Olivia, gift and commitment. May you have a long and fortunate life.

ACKNOWLEDGEMENTS

To all divisionarios and their relatives who made this book possible, to the Blue Division Foundation, which keeps the spirit of the divisionarios alive. To the Retógenes Association, and to the Don Rodrigo Foundation. To Pedro Aibar, Jaime Barriuso, Paloma Bengoechea Martí, Carlos Caballero, Jesus Dolado, Alfonso Escuadra, Jesús Gómez Gómez-Jareño, Juan Negreira, Manuel Pérez Rubio, Antonio Prieto Barrio, Jaime Sadurní, Alfonso Ruiz de Castro, Luis Miguel Sánchez Pérez, Ramón Sierra Martín-Portugués, Pablo Larraz Andía, and Santiago Guillén García.

HITLER'S SPANISH DIVISION

Pablo Sagarra • Óscar González • Lucas Molina

Illustrations: Ramiro Bujeiro

FRONTLINE BOOKS

Hitler's Spanish Division

First published in Great Britain in 2019 by

FRONTLINE BOOKS
An imprint of
Pen & Sword Books Ltd
Yorkshire - Philadelphia

Copyright © Pablo Sagarra, Óscar González, Lucas Molina

ISBN 978 1 47387 887 7

The right of Pablo Sagarra, Óscar González and Lucas Molinato be identified as
Author of this work has been asserted by them in accordance
with the Copyright, Designs and Patents Act 1988.

A CIP catalogue record for this book is
available from the British Library

All rights reserved. No part of this book may be reproduced or
transmitted in any form or by any means, electronic or mechanical
including photocopying, recording or by any information storage and
retrieval system, without permission from the Publisher in writing.

Typeset in 9.5/13 Palatino
by Aura Technology and Software Services, India
Printed and bound by Replika Press, India

Pen & Sword Books Ltd incorporates the Imprints of Aviation, Atlas,
Family History, Fiction, Maritime, Military, Discovery, Politics, History,
Archaeology, Select, Wharncliffe Local History, Wharncliffe True Crime,
Military Classics, Wharncliffe Transport, Leo Cooper, The Praetorian Press,
Remember When, Seaforth Publishing and Frontline Publishing.

For a complete list of Pen & Sword titles please contact
PEN & SWORD BOOKS LTD
47 Church Street, Barnsley, South Yorkshire, S70 2AS, England
E-mail: enquiries@pen-and-sword.co.uk
Website: www.pen-and-sword.co.uk

Or
PEN AND SWORD BOOKS
1950 Lawrence Rd, Havertown, PA 19083, USA
E-mail: Uspen-and-sword@casematepublishers.com
Website: www.penandswordbooks.com

CONTENTS

Introduction	7
Generals	15
Colonels	19
Lieutenant Colonels	23
Majors	27
Liaison Staff	35
Junior Officers	39
Ncos	47
Ncos and Men	55
Men	59
Blue Legion	71
Last Volunteers	75
Blue Squadron	79
Navy and Todt Organization	89
Services	93
Diplomats	105
Post-War	109

'Torres de nuestro honor, como raíces,
Aras ocultas, templos entrañados,
Semillas de extremada primavera
Y noches que atestiguan como auroras.
Fundadores de tierra: territorio de España,
Nuevo aquí, bajo la nieve.'

'Towers of our honour, like roots,
Hidden altars, deep temples,
Seeds of extreme spring
And nights that stand witness like dawns.
Founders of land: territory of Spain,
New here, under the snow.'
(A letter to my friends from Novgorod cemetery, in spring
Cuadernos de Rusia. Dionisio Ridruejo).

'Revolucionando las leyes de la naturaleza,
El león vive y ruge en los glaciares rusos por primera vez.
Es el León Hispano, ¡es la gloriosa tradición de nuestra Infantería!'

'Turning the laws of nature upside down,
The lion lives and roars on the Russian glaciers for the first time.
It's the Spanish lion, it's the glorious tradition of our infantry!'
(Luis Aparicio, Blue Division. Notas de un diario
La Joven Europa, Cuaderno 5, May 1942).

Buena fama merece quien por su patria muere

Those who die for their country deserve high reputation
(Spanish saying).

INTRODUCTION

The story of the 250th Division of the *Wehrmacht*, the Spanish Blue Division, as told by its former members, by historians, by writers, and by film and documentary makers, continues to captivate the public at large. The three-year campaign in which the Blue Division fought was one of the most dramatic and memorable events of the Second World War.

The division was created at the start of Operation *Barbarossa*, the invasion of the Soviet Union by Germany. The Third Reich accepted the Spanish government's offer to send an expeditionary force to fight against the Red Army. In the words of Víctor de la Serna, journalist and volunteer on the Russian front, 'The Blue Division did not go to Russia in a quest for *Lebensraum*, or in search of territorial dominance, or to extend the borders of Spain that Spain did not have. It went to ratify, on behalf of our homeland, as did no other country of the so-called free world, its claim that communism was wrong and its resolve to fight against it to the death.'

In July 1941, 18,000 volunteers, servicemen and Falangists enlisted in the army of the Reich. After training at Grafenwöhr (Bavaria), on 12 October 1941, they arrived, ready

and eager to fight, at the Volkhov sector, where Hitler's war machine was grinding to a halt on the Russian front. The Spanish Air Force and Navy also sent volunteers. Spanish pilots and ground crews formed the five Blue Squadrons that fought in the central sector of the eastern front, and Spanish seamen formed two reserve detachments which, in 1942, were quietly absorbed into the *Kriegsmarine*.

The campaign in the first winter was gruelling. The *Wehrmacht* suffered major losses and the Russian weather wrought havoc among the front-line troops. In northern Russia, close to the 60th parallel where the Spanish were deployed, temperatures were brutally low, under minus 40°C. The following year, after the annihilation of the Volkhov Pocket, the Blue Division was transferred to the Leningrad front. By then the bulk of the unit had been replaced by reinforcements from Spain to cover casualties and to relieve the veterans of the previous summer.

The second winter was milder in terms of the weather but hostilities were even more intense. Among other battles, the period saw the Battle of Krasny, which began on 10 February 1943. That day the Blue Division, supported by German units, withstood the heaviest attack of the campaign thus far in terms of the colossal firepower and offensive capabilities brought to bear by the enemy, at a cost of a sea of casualties and the loss of a handful of kilometres of ground. The Spanish troops continued to fight in a thankless and inglorious positional

THE SPANISH CAMPAIGN IN RUSSIA 1941-1944

Some 48,000 volunteers participated in the campaign, including 659 men in the Luftwaffe, 134 in the *Kriegsmarine* and approximately 1,000 in the *Waffen SS* and other units of the *Wehrmacht* and the Organization Todt.

A number of awards and decorations were made. Of the main Spanish decorations, there were eight awards of the Royal and Military Order of Saint Ferdinand, sixty-nine of the *Medalla Militar* (of which fifty-three were to men in the Division and sixteen to those serving in the air element), and two *Medalla Militar Colectiva*.

In terms of German decorations, there were two awards of the Knight's Cross of the Iron Cross (*Ritterkreuz* – one with Oak Leaves), three *Deutsches Kreuz in Gold*, around 165 Iron Crosses First Class, and approximately 2,500 Iron Crosses Second Class.

Roughly 53% of the Spanish personnel were casualties. This total includes 5,000 men who were killed, 9,000 who were injured, 400 who were captured and became prisoners of war in the USSR (of whom about 125 died in captivity), seventy who deserted, and 250 who were reported missing.

PABLO SAGARRA - ÓSCAR GONZÁLEZ - LUCAS MOLINA

war until they were repatriated in the autumn of 1943. Around two thousand troops stayed on with the Blue Legion to continue the fight in the Kostovo sector at Lyuban until April 1944 when they too returned to Spain. At around this time the last of the airmen, members of the 5th Blue Squadron, also returned home. The Spanish campaign in Russia was over, although some anti-communist volunteers enlisted in the *Wehrmacht* and continued to fight on their own account until Germany fell in May 1945.

The Blue Division is a fascinating subject for historians and readers all over the world, one which has generated a vast and seemingly never-ending bibliography. There are all kinds of books of varying literary merit about this great unit, written from a political, diplomatic, social or military viewpoint. There are both general studies and more focused ones, for example, on the volunteers from one particular province or region of Spain or dealing with a specific unit or service. There are also books analysing the structure, uniform, equipment and weapons of the volunteers, the medals they were awarded, or the battles they fought or their theatres of operations.

However, in this panoply of publications there was none that presented the *divisionarios* with their authentic uniform in an artistic and entertaining manner. We use the terms artistic, entertaining and authentic because up to now, and without detracting from their merit, the studies of uniforms that have directly or tangentially dealt with the Blue Division did so, as is normally the case in specialist publications on this subject (both Spanish and non-Spanish), in such a technical and dry manner that, in addition to losing touch with the historical reality of the uniforms of the Spanish volunteers, they run the risk of leaving their readers cold.

There are already very comprehensive studies of the German uniforms and equipment used by the Spanish troops who fought under the flag of the Third Reich. This book is not then a treatise on the uniforms of the Blue Division; it is a book about *divisionarios* and their uniforms. This is not wordplay; they are two radically different approaches to the same subject.

The raison d'être of this book is the volunteer; the individual Spaniards who historically wore those uniforms. Because beneath each *Wehrmacht* cap there was a head that thought and under each Wehrmacht tunic there was a heart that beat and felt. There was a person of flesh and bone, with a past and a present, with a profoundly Spanish identity and character, all of which needs to be given full consideration. This book is about the men and women who served in the Russian campaign, above all else.

The true, unique personality and background of each Spanish combatant was reflected in their uniforms, however much this scandalized the Germans and a few of their more regulation-abiding fellow Spaniards. The inevitable contact with the Russian populace and customs, the climate, and the local culture naturally had an influence on the *divisionarios* too.

It is therefore necessary to reflect the reality of the situation; although the Blue Division volunteers used German uniforms and equipment, they always did so in a recognizably Spanish way. The cocktail of Spanishness and German uniform regulations could not fail to produce a special kind of soldier, the *divisionario*, whose uniform and military style was far removed from those established for the *Wehrmacht*. This book aims to contextualize and document the Blue Division volunteers' habit of flouting the rules by wearing non-regulation badges, decorations, articles of clothing, and all kinds of other non-military or political bits and bobs. The flipside of the *divisionarios'* need to express their Spanishness was that when the campaign was over, civilians and servicemen alike would go home laden with items of German uniforms.

We have studied individual volunteers through an extraordinary collection of illustrations by Ramiro Bujeiro, the father of war art and one of the best illustrators in the world. The Argentine artist depicts real *divisionarios* with the rank, weapons and duties they would have had at various periods of the campaign. He includes volunteers who served in the *Luftwaffe* and in the *Kriegsmarine* and a number of Spanish and non-Spanish military, civil or diplomatic staff related to the great unit. Also featured in this book are, of course, a number of veterans of the Russian front wearing the Spanish Army uniforms used after 1940.

What follows is the most serious analysis made to date of the real uniforms worn by the volunteers of the Blue Division and the Blue Squadrons. The plasticity and peerless style of Ramiro Bujeiro's illustrations, based on the work of a team of researchers and with the support of the families and friends of the men, and experts in uniformology, is enriched by explanatory text and a large number of photographs, most of which were previously unpublished.

Note: To avoid having ranks expressed in Spanish when referring to the Civil War and after Second World War, and in German when referring to the Blue Division, Legion and Squadron, leading to a plethora of foreign words which might interfere with reader's enjoyment of the book, in the body of the text equivalent English ranks have been used at all times, while in the photo and illustration captions the relevant Spanish and German ranks are mostly maintained.

Generalleutnant Agustín Muñoz Grandes, Commander of the Blue Division; December 1942.

General de División Emilio Esteban-Infantes Martín, Commander of the Blue Division; December 1943.

Generalmajor Santiago Amado Lóriga, Commander of the Blue Division; November 1943.

GENERALS

The three generals who led the Blue Division were gritty soldiers. Originally infantry officers and veterans of the Rif War[1], they were all battle-hardened in the 1936-1939 Civil War.

Agustín Muñoz Grandes, the youngest of the three, was born in Carabanchel Bajo (Madrid) on 27 January 1896. He was a dyed-in-the-wool *africanista*, having served in Morocco for many years. He commanded the Assault Guard Corps in the 2nd Republic, and in the Civil War he commanded the 2nd Navarra Brigade, the

Above. From left to right, Teniente Coronel Cárcer, General Muñoz Grandes and Teniente Coronel Pérez-Íñigo (side on). *(José Pérez-Íñigo Delgado family archive)*

Below. General Muñoz Grandes wearing the uniform of the head of Franco's military household on returning from Russia. *(Ramón Sampietro archive)*

150th Division, and the Urgel Army Corps, among other units. As Commander-in-Chief of the Blue Division until December 1942, it was he who gave that great unit its style of combat which so surprised and then impressed the German high command. Back in Spain he would continue to further his military career while moving into politics, becoming Minister of the Army and then Vice-President of the Government. He died with the rank of Captain General in Madrid on 11 July 1970.

In Ramiro Bujeiro's illustration he is wearing the uniform of a lieutenant general, with a type 38

The German general Friedrich Wilhelm von Chappuis, head of the XXXVIII Army Corps, together with the Spanish general Muñoz Grandes. *(Palomino File Fariñas).*

---

1 The Rif War was fought in the Rif Mountains of Morocco between Franco-Spanish forces and local Berber tribes between 1920 and 1927.

Franco at the El Pardo Palace. Behind him, among other generals and admirals, is Muñoz Grandes wearing the uniform of Franco's Military Household. At his throat he is wearing the Knight's Cross with Oak Leaves which he won in Russia. *(Ramón Sampietro archive)*

side-cap and sporting 1st and 2nd Class Iron Crosses and the Knight's Cross with Oak Leaves.

Emilio Esteban-Infantes Martín, born in Toledo on 18 May 1892, fought at Larache in 1913 in the same regiment as Muñoz Grandes, the 40th Covadonga, after which he joined the General Staff Corps. He was expelled from the army after the rebellion on 10 August 1932, before returning to active service at the outbreak of the Civil War, in which he distinguished himself as a magnificent Chief of Staff in the Castile Army Corps. He organized the relief of the Blue Division in March 1942; in June he travelled to Berlin and after various diplomatic vicissitudes he arrived at the front in August as second-in-command of the division until relieving Muñoz Grandes. Thanks to his leadership, among other factors, the Battle of Krasny-Bor was a resounding defensive victory for the Spanish troops. He went on to occupy a number of important positions in the army before dying in Gijón with the rank of lieutenant general on September 5, 1962.

He has been sketched in the Spanish uniform with which he was repatriated in December 1943. Note the general's red sash, his German medals (Knight's Cross and the German Cross in Gold), and the Spanish Individual Military Medal. His

Above. German General Philipp Kleffel, head of the I Army Corps, with General Esteban-Infantes. *(Esteban-Infantes family)*

Left. Award of decorations to a group of Spanish soldiers of the 2nd/262nd Regiment. Erik-Oskar Hansen, General-in-Chief of the LIV Army Corps is speaking into a microphone. On the left is Emilio Esteban-Infantes. *(Esteban-Infantes family)*

Lunch at the Blue Division Headquarters. General Esteban-Infantes is addressing those seated around the table. *(Esteban-Infantes family)*

uniform is the same as the one which he wore when he joined the Blue Division in June 1942, a habitual practice among all *divisionarios*, whose appurtenances were stored by the quartermaster. It should be noted that Esteban Infantes had been made a lieutenant general by battlefield promotion on May 26 of that same year.

Santiago Amado Lóriga was born in La Coruña on April 12, 1890. He belonged to the same class of the Spanish Infantry Academy as Esteban-Infantes, Franco, and Yagüe. He fought in Africa and in the Civil War, in the latter earning the Individual Military Medal while in command of the *Bandera*[2] *Sanjurjo*. He received a bullet wound in the face at Sierra Alcubierre. While Director (Colonel) of the Infantry Academy at Zaragoza he joined the Blue Division, in which he commanded the 263rd Regiment until his promotion to brigadier in October 1943, serving as infantry commander and second-in-command of the division. For a few days in November he commanded the Blue Division, overseeing its definitive disbandment and

the formation of the Blue Legion. After repatriation he continued to pursue his military career until he died in Zaragoza on 31 January 1974, with the rank of lieutenant general.

He is seen on page 14 wearing the regulation uniform of the *Wehrmacht* with a peaked cap and the collar patches of a major general. He is wearing an Individual Military Medal and an Iron Cross 2nd Class, hung in the Spanish manner.

Centre. General Santiago Amado Lóriga, having recently been awarded the Iron Cross 2nd Class.

Below. Santiago Amado Lóriga among Spanish visitors to a Tiger I tank unit. *(Francisco Arnaiz archive)*

---

2 A *bandera* of the Spanish Legion was the equivalent of a battalion. The Spanish term is used throughout the book, and any mention of the Legion (rather than the Blue Legion) refers to the Spanish military formation, *La Legión Española*.

Coronel Francisco Bandín Delgado, Commander of the 10th Marching Battalion; June 1942.

Oberst José Vierna Trápaga, Commander of the 263rd Infantry Regiment; May 1942.

Oberst Miguel Rodrigo Martínez, Blue Division Infantry Commander, 1941.

COLONELS

Of the sixteen colonels who served in the Blue Division, including the two who acted as rear services commanders, Luis Pumarola Alaiz and Manuel González de Jonte y Corradi, we have chosen three, all born in the nineteenth century and all Rif War veterans.

Miguel Rodrigo Martínez, a war orphan, was born in Santa Clara (Cuba) on 27 December 1895. A man of exceptional bravery, he came away from the African and Civil War campaigns with two Individual Military Medals and the Individual Laureate Cross of Saint Ferdinand for the part he played at the head of the

Coronel Rodrigo, with Muñoz Grandes, talking to German officers; October 1941 (Pérez-Íñigo family archive)

Miguel Rodrigo, holder of the Laureate Cross of Saint Ferdinand and the Military Medal, photographed when he was a general in 1959. (Arcadio Carrasco archive)

3rd Company, 2nd *Tabor*[1] of the 2nd *Melilla* Regular Forces Group in the relief of Kudia Tahar, a key position close to Tetuan, on 9 September 1925. After the regiment he commanded was disbanded at Grafenwöhr, he became second-in-command of the Blue Division and commander of its infantry, and late in the campaign he took over the command of the 269th Regiment from the repatriated Martínez-Esparza. He died in Madrid on 5 November 1968 with the rank of lieutenant general.

He is depicted in the uniform of a colonel (*oberst*) in the *Wehrmacht*, wearing the Laureate Cross of Saint Ferdinand.

José Vierna Trápaga, born in Colindres (Santander) on October 28, 1888. Another *africanista*, he served for a long time in the Spanish Legion, among other units. While in the 4th Bandera he was awarded the Collective Laureate Cross of Saint Ferdinand

---

[1] A *tabor* was a unit of indigenous Moroccan troops, the equivalent of a battalion.

Coronel Rodrigo, a heavy smoker, with Blue Division commanders and officers; October 1941. *(Juan Negreira archive)*

for the capture of Badajoz in August 1936. He also held two Individual Military Medals. He joined the Blue Division as a lieutenant colonel and was made a colonel by battlefield promotion on his arrival in Germany. He commanded the 263rd Regiment until his repatriation in June 1942. He rose to the rank of lieutenant general in reserve before dying on 23 February 1976.

In the illustration we can see the collar of his blue shirt worn outside his tunic, and his Iron Cross 1st Class awarded on April 18, 1942.

Francisco Bandín Delgado was born in Mula (Murcia) on 27 September 1884. As an artillery captain he took part in the Alhucemas landing as artillery commander of Colonel Mola's column and of the Melilla vanguard zone. He spent the Civil War in Madrid; either in prison, in the Finnish embassy, or hidden in a safe house. As colonel of the 48th Artillery Regiment

Above and right. Two photographs of José Vierna Trápaga at the Russian Front. *(Vierna family archive)*

Left. General Martínez de Campos (middle) walking next to Esteban-Infantes in Puschkin on 5 May 1943. To the left of the photograph is the then *Coronel* Bandín. *(Esteban-Infantes family archive)*

Coronel Bandín on the day he left Spain bound for Germany, 12 June 1942.

garrisoned at La Coruña, in March 1942 he was given the task of organizing the relief of the Blue Division artillery. He arrived at the Russian front in the summer as commander of the 250th Artillery Regiment, a post he held until the following year. One of his two sons, Luis Fernando, also fought in the Russian campaign, being wounded at Possad while serving as an infantry second lieutenant in the 2nd/269th. Francisco Bandín reached the rank of brigadier, was transferred to the reserve in 1948, and died in Madrid on November 16, 1967.

On page 18 he is shown wearing the uniform he wore when he left Spain at the head of the 10th Marching Battalion, which crossed the Spanish-French border on 12 June 1942. On his collar, above the artillery badge, we see the gold five-pointed star awarded to those holding a General Staff Diploma (he belonged to the same class as Esteban-Infantes). On his head is a red beret with the three stars of a colonel, and among his accoutrements are leather belts (*trinchas*), paste buttons, a pen and a whistle.

Above, below and left. Three photographs of José Vierna Trápaga, two of them at the Russian Front and the third wearing the summer uniform of a general back in Spain in the 1960s. As we can see he is wearing the Iron Cross 1st Class and a battlefield promotion badge along with his Military Medal. (Vierna family archive)

Oberstleutnant José Canillas Hernández-Helena, Second-in-Command of the 263rd Infantry Regiment; winter 1941-42.

Oberstleutnant Mariano Gómez-Zamalloa Quirce, Second-in-Command of the 262nd Infantry Regiment; April 1942.

Teniente Coronel Ramón Rodríguez Vita, Commander of the 4th Repatriation Battalion; July 1942.

LIEUTENANT COLONELS

In Russia there were thirty-six Spanish lieutenant colonels (thirty joined the division at this rank and six majors were promoted during the campaign), normally acting as second-in-command or adjutant or performing other services appropriate to their rank. We have chosen three who served in fighting units.

José Canillas Hernández-Helena, born in Zamora on 6 March 1891, fought in Morocco until 1915 in what would be the legendary 69th Africa Infantry Regiment.

When the Second Republic was established he left the Army, returning to active service during the repression of the Asturian rebellion in 1934. The Civil War caught him by surprise in Murcia and he had an eventful journey back to the Nationalist Zone. He fought with distinction at Brunete and on the Toledo front, being wounded twice. He joined the Blue Division as second-in-command of the 263rd Regiment. He was awarded the Iron Cross 1st Class before returning to Spain in October 1942. He remained in the Army and died in Madrid as a brigadier (retired) on 18 January 1968.

Teniente Coronel Canillas driving a sled on the Volkhov Front; winter 1941-42.

The illustration shows him at Nikitkino, at the Volkhov bridgehead, in December 1941, when he was commanding an ad hoc combat unit called the *Agrupación Oriental* (the Eastern Group, aka the *Agrupación Canillas*, after its original commander) at the southernmost end of the Spanish deployment in that sector. He is wearing a sheepskin overcoat and a regulation sidecap, while protecting himself from the cold with a non-military scarf.

Canillas on horseback on the Russian Front.

Wehrmacht breast eagle and Iron Cross 2nd Class belonging to Gómez Zamalloa. *(Gómez-Zamalloa family archive)*

The then *Oberstleutnant* Gómez Zamalloa, wearing a German uniform displaying his Laureate and Individual Military Medal earned in the Spanish Civil War. *(Gómez-Zamalloa family archive)*

Mariano Gómez-Zamalloa Quirce was born in La Coruña on 26 March 1897. As a young officer he fought in Morocco in the 1st Tetuan and 3rd Ceuta Regular Forces Groups. With the 2nd *Tabor* of the latter group he crossed the Strait of Gibraltar to begin his Civil War campaign on the mainland, during which he was wounded a number of times and awarded medals for heroism. In the Blue Division he served as second-in-command of the 262nd Regiment until his repatriation in May 1942. He also lived through the Sidi-Ifni war as governor of the province of Spanish West Africa (and of the province of Ifni from January 1958). He died as a lieutenant general in the reserve in Madrid, on September 4, 1973.

He is shown on page 22 with the regulation uniform of a lieutenant colonel (*oberstleutnant*). He is wearing the Individual Military Medal and the Laureate Cross of Saint Ferdinand, medals that he won in the Civil War for taking and heroically defending enemy trenches on Pingarrón Hill on the Jarama front in February 1937, when his *Tabor* was heavily outnumbered by Republican forces. He received six bullet wounds and nine shrapnel injuries, after which he was carried from the battlefield unconscious.

Ceremony held in Ceuta at which Comandante Gómez-Zamalloa was awarded the Laureate Cross of Saint Ferdinand. He is wearing the cordons of an ADC of the Deputy Inspector General of the First Military Region, the post he held at that time *(Gómez-Zamalloa family archive)*

General Gómez-Zamalloa shaking the hand of the Head of State, Francisco Franco, in the early 1970s. *(Gómez-Zamalloa family archive)*

He is wearing, in the correct manner, the ribbon of the Iron Cross 2nd Class which he was awarded on 27 April 1942.

Ramón Rodríguez Vita was born in Granada on 23 February 1902. He was one of several brothers and brothers-in-law serving in Africa as artillerymen in the last throes of the Rif War in 1927. He retired from the army in 1931 to work in the state-owned oil company CAMPSA until returning to active service on the outbreak of the Civil War. In Russia he served as commander of the 1st Light Artillery Group and, after his promotion to lieutenant colonel, as second-in-command of the 250th Artillery Regiment. He rose to the rank of lieutenant general and held the position of Captain General of Madrid, among other posts. He died in Madrid on 12 September 1989.

Rodríguez Vita is depicted on page 22 in San Sebastian Sebastián, on Sunday 12 July 1942, when he arrived in Spain as the commander of the 4th Repatriation Battalion. He is wearing the uniform that the *divisionarios* returned to Spain in, with a blue shirt, black tie and gloves. He is also wearing an Iron Cross 1st Class, Falangist arrows on his right-hand breast pocket, and the Individual Military Medal he earned at Reus, on 4 January 1939, while commanding the 105/11 Light Artillery Group forming part of the 5th Navarra Division.

Above. Rodríguez Vita on his return from the Russian Front at Irún railway station.

Left. Wound chevrons. Rodríguez Vita was wounded on two occasions before joining the Blue Division.

Right. Teniente Coronel Rodríguez Vita at Grigorovo about to start his journey home. *(Martínez Cattáneo family archive)*

Major Guillermo Reinlein Calzada, Commander of the I/250th Artillery Regiment; February 1943.

Major Manuel García Andino, Commander 3rd Section of the General Staff; June 1943.

Major Manuel de Mora-Figueroa y Gómez-Imaz, Adjutant to General Muñoz Grandes; spring 1942.

MAJORS

A total 137 majors served in the Blue Division and in the Blue Squadrons (including the eleven captains who were promoted to this rank during the campaign), among whom was the legendary Miguel Román Garrido. The heroic 2nd Battalion of the 263rd Regiment became known as the Román Battalion in his honour. We will be looking at six other majors of the Blue Division in their various postings.

Grigorovo, spring 1942. *Comandante* Mora-Figueroa chatting with a fellow major, Homar Servera, and other Blue Division officers. *(Pérez-Íñigo family archive)*

Manuel de Mora-Figueroa y Gómez-Imaz belonged to an aristocratic Andalusian family with seafaring roots. He was born in Sevilla on 4 October 1904. His first campaign was in Africa where he served as a navy sub lieutenant on the gunboat *Bonifaz*. The Civil War found him retired from the Navy in Cadiz, but on 18 July, with a group fellow-countrymen and Falangists, he took part in the successful uprising in that provincial capital city. Being a naval lieutenant, he needed little encouragement to organize and lead a group of volunteers in Cadiz, the *Tercio Mora-Figueroa*, with which he fought on several fronts, receiving the Individual Military Medal for his actions at Villanueva del Duque in March 1937.

Capitán de Corbeta Mora-Figueroa was a marine who had earned the Individual Military Medal in the Spanish Civil War for his actions in the Villanueva del Duque sector in March 1937.

He was the civil governor of Madrid when he joined the Blue Division where he served as adjutant to General Muñoz Grandes. He went on to have a number of bureaucratic postings before dying in Madrid as a rear admiral in the Spanish Navy on 13 January 1964.

Nothing about Mora-Figueroa's German uniform denotes that he was the only naval officer who served in the Blue Division. On his breast he wears the Individual Military Medal and the ribbon of the Iron Cross 2nd Class, and on his sleeve the shield of the *Falange Española de las Juntas de Ofensiva Nacional-Sindicalista* (hereinafter *FE de las JONS*), the national syndicalist organization to which he had belonged since 1934.

On the far right of the photo, Mora-Figueroa stands at the end of the line with Muñoz Grandes and Rodrigo, among others. *(De Rojas family archive)*

Manuel García Andino was born in Rio-Piedras, Puerto Rico on 11 August 1898. He fought in the Rif War in 1923 and 1924 as a cavalry officer, serving in a squadron of the 5th Alhucemas Regular Forces Group. He was transferred to the General Staff Corps and during the Civil War served as Chief of Staff in the 2nd Castilla Brigade and in the 62nd Division (Sagardía). In the Blue Division he served on the General Staff, most of the time as commander of the 3rd Section (Operations), although he also held a provisional post for several

Above. The then *Coronel* García Andino at an anniversary mass for his comrade-at-arms who died in Russia, Comandante José Alemany. *(García Andino family archive)*

Right. In the foreground, García Andino, at Pokrovskaya in July 1943. The crimson stripes of the trousers worn by General Staff officers can clearly be seen. *(García Andino family archive)*

Right. García Andino, third from the left. In the photo we can also see *Comandante* Sanchón (first from the left), Coronel García Navarro (fourth from the left), and *Comandante* Alemany (fifth from the left) *(Juan Negreira archive)*

months as Head of the General Staff. While still active, holding the rank of colonel and serving in the Army riding school, he died in Medina de Pomar (Burgos) on 3 October 1955.

In the illustration García Andino is shown with the uniform trousers of a General Staff officer, wearing the ribbons of the Iron Cross 2nd Class and the Iron Cross 1st Class.

Guillermo Reinlein Calzada was born in Caravaca (Murcia) on 24 August 1901. He saw action in Morocco in various artillery units and when the 18 July rebellion broke out in 1936, he played an active part in it. He went out onto the streets of Barcelona at the head of two columns from the San Andrés barracks and headed for the city centre where he engaged regular troops and militia loyal to the Republic. He was wounded, arrested, tried and sentenced, seeing out the rest of the war in prison. In Russia he served as commander of the 1st Artillery Group and, after his promotion to lieutenant colonel, as adjutant to

Reinlein being awarded the Individual Military Medal for his conduct at Krasny Bor.

Visit in September 1943 by a Blue Division commission to the *Generalkommisar* of the Reich in Estonia, *SA-Obergruppenfuhrer* Karl Sigismund Litzmann. Reinlein (fifth from the left, with glasses) was among those present. From left to right: Ackermann, Metternich, Esteban-Infantes, [unknown], Reinlein, Litzmann and Knüppel.
(Juan Negreira archive)

Left. Propaganda postcards, medals, and a copy of *Hoja de Campaña*, the Blue Division's newspaper. *(Jaime Sadurní collection)*

in Madrid, when the Civil War broke out it caught him in a Nationalist Zone. He fought with the García Escámez column, was a trainer in an academy for acting second lieutenants, and commanded a number of mixed groups of engineers specializing in fortifications. In the Blue Division he General Esteban-Infantes. He died in Barcelona, shortly after returning from Russia, on 17 July 1947.

Bujeiro depicts Reinlein on page 26 with the winter uniform of the *Wehrmacht*, with regulation boots and parka and a Russian-style cap. He is unshaven as he had just taken part in the Battle of Krasny-Bor in which he distinguished himself in command of his batteries and men, receiving the Individual Military Medal in recognition of his performance.

Alfredo Bellod Gómez, was born on 14 January 1899, in Calahorra (Logroño). He served in Africa as a sapper and in a signals company. Although he was stationed

Below. Comandante Bellod in the winter of 1942; Leningrad Front. *(Bellod family archive)*

Above. Bellod with his engineer officer's uniform before the Spanish Civil War. *(Bellod family archive)*

Left. Alfredo Bellod with three officers of his staff at Novgorod; summer 1942. *(Bellod family archive)*

commanded the 25th Assault Sapper Battalion between May 1942 and April 1943, a unit with which he distinguished himself at the Battle of Krasny-Bor.

On returning to Spain he stayed on in the Army, rising to the rank of brigadier. He died at the ripe old age of 100 in Madrid, on 1 August 1999.

In the illustration he is seen in the summer of 1942 wearing the uniform of a sapper.

General Bellod at his family home wearing a Spanish uniform displaying the medals he won during the various campaigns he took part in. (Bellod family archive)

He is relaxed, without a sash, and is pictured in front of the domes of the Saint Sophia Cathedral in the Novgorod Kremlin, where the Headquarter Company of his unit was stationed. He is wearing no medals because his 2nd and 1st Class Iron Crosses were awarded at a later date.

Ángel Sánchez del Águila Menco was born in Madrid on 31 March 1897. He fought in Morocco with squadrons of the Cazadores de Alcántara Regiment, the 14th Cavalry, and the 1st Tetuan Regular Forces Group. During his service in Africa he rose to the rank of captain by battlefield promotion. At the start of the Civil War he was incarcerated in the military prison of Castillo de San Carlos in Palma de Mallorca. On his release he fought in the 1st Cavalry Division, among other units. He was the first commander of the Blue Division's Exploration Group, and returned to Spain sporting an Iron Cross 2nd Class. He stayed in the army until he retired in March 1959, with the honorary rank of cavalry colonel. We have no record of when he died.

Above. Comandante *Sánchez del Águila* and Comandante *Homar on the Volkhov Front; winter 1941-42. (Juan Negreira archive)*

Below. *In a photo which shows the cold they had to endure,* Comandante *Sánchez del Águila is wearing ear muffs to prevent frostbite. (De Rojas family archive)*

He is shown on page 30 on the Volkhov front wearing a heavy winter overcoat and the typical headgear of the Wehrmacht, with the yellow gold piping of the cavalry.

Tomás García Rebull was born in Vinaroz (Castellón) on 21 February 1907. He fought in Africa (5th Alhucemas Regular Forces Group and the Mehal-la[1] de Yebala at Xauen) and took part in the July 18

---

1 A *mehal-la* was the name given to a unit of indigenous troops in Morocco. It was the equivalent of a (small) regiment and consisted of a number of *tabores* (battalions).

rebellion in Tarragona. He was arrested by government authorities and sent to a Republican battalion on the Granada front, where he made his escape to the Nationalist Zone. In September 1938, during the Battle of the Ebro, he won the Individual Military Medal at the head of the 5th Bandera of the *Falange Española Tradicionalista y de las Juntas de Ofensiva Nacional Sindicalista* (hereinafter *FET y de las JONS*, the result of the merger of the *FE de las Jons* with the Carlist Party in 1937) of Navarra. In the Blue Division he was commander-in-chief of the 1st Battalion of the 269th Regiment, where he won his second Individual Military Medal for his memorable defence of Possad. After repatriation in December 1942, he remained in the Army, reaching the rank of lieutenant general and continued to be an active member of the National Movement (aka FET y de las JONS). He died on 28 April 1976.

Left. García Rebull early in the 1980s, wearing the uniform of a *Teniente General*. His last active service posting was at the Captaincy General of the First Military region *(Madrid)*. *(García Rebull family archive)*

Below. Mass in Russia. A few paces behind the priest, semi-obscured by a branch, is *Comandante* García Rebull. *(García Rebull family archive)*

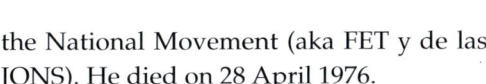

Bujeiro depicts him as an infantry major around the autumn of 1942 with the German medals won in the previous winter's fighting. He is one of the few Blue Division commanders who was a *camisa vieja* (literally 'old shirt'; a member of the original Falangist movement) who had secretly joined the *FE de las JONS* in 1934. Here he proudly displays the Falangist yoke and arrows badge, which he wore throughout the rest of his life.

Left above. The then Mayor of Madrid, Carlos Arias Navarro, standing next to *Teniente General* Tomás García Rebull. Also in the photo, from left to right, are the Civil Governor of Burgos, Federico Trillo Figueroa and Air Force *Teniente General,* Miguel Guerrero García, who is sporting an Individual Military Medal and an Air Medal. The photo was taken in the early 1970s. *(García Rebull family archive)*

Left. Medals belonging to *Teniente General* Tomás García Rebull. *(García Rebull family archive)*

Oberst Antonio García Navarro, Commander of the Spanish Legion of Volunteers; March 1944.

Oberst Wilhelm von Knüppel, Commander of the German Liaison Staff, May 1943.

Oberleutnant Paul A. Metternich-Winneburg, Interpreter for the Liaison Staff; November 1943.

LIAISON STAFF

The 250th Division had an attached unit, the Liaison Staff, to facilitate communication within the *Wehrmacht*, manned by Germans who acted mainly as translators and advisors. Two of its members are shown here, accompanied by Colonel (*Oberst*) García Navarro.

Wilhelm Knüppel was born in Suckow an der Ihna, Pomerania, on 12 November 1902. He joined the *Reichswehr* (German National Defence) as a cadet in 1922 at the age of twenty, and fought in the Second World War, firstly in command of the 483rd Infantry Regiment and later as Chief of Staff of the 246th Division, before being

Above. Knüppel, in the middle of the photo, in conference with Almirante Canaris, head of the Abwehr, and Generals Esteban-Infantes and Martínez de Campos, on the visit made by the latter to the General HQ of the Blue Division; May 1943. *(Juan Negreira archive)*

Left. *From left to right:* Wilhelm von Knüppel, Guillermo Reinlein and Emilio Esteban-Infantes; Estonia, September 1943. *(Juan Negreira archive)*

transferred to the Liaison Staff of the Blue Division. He served in a number of other units before the German capitulation in May 1945, by which time he had risen to the rank of brigadier. He died in Koblenz on 16 September 1968.

On his colonel's uniform he wears, among other decorations, the prestigious *Blutorden* (Blood Order) ribbon which was awarded to members of the NSDAP (Nazi Party) who had taken part in the Munich Putsch of 1923 or supported the movement prior to Hitler's rise to power in January 1933. He also sports the Iron

Cross 1st Class and the Spanish *Cruz de Guerra* (War Cross).

Paul Alfons von Metternich-Winneburg, son of Isabel de Silva y Carvajal, Marchioness of Castillejo, and the Rhine Prince Klemens von Metternich, was born in Vienna on 26 May 1917. Born into the aristocracy, he married Princess Tatiana Vassiltchikova, daughter of Russian aristocrats and a direct descendent of Tsar Alexander. He served as an interpreter in the Liaison staff of the Blue Division and later in the Blue Legion between 1943 and 1944. After the war he ran a winery and became a racing driver, going on to become president of world motorsport's governing body, the FIA, a post he held for ten years. He died in Geneva on 21 September 1992.

He is shown on page 34 wearing the uniform of a lieutenant (*oberleutnant*) with a buttoned overcoat.

Knüppel in a horse-drawn carriage accompanied by Ackermann and other officers. *(Juan Negreira archive)*

Left. Work meeting. Esteban-Infantes and *Generalfeldmarschall* Georg von Küchler, commander of Army Group North. Prince Metternich is acting as interpreter and *Oberst* Knüppel is standing behind them. *(Juan Negreira archive)*

Below. Prince Metternich, third from the left, next to *Teniente Coronel* Robles Pazos and other Spanish officers. *(Robles Pazos family archive)*

Above. Prince Metternich and General Helmuth Priess, of the 121st Infantry Division talking to a Spanish foot soldier. *(Sáenz de Cabezón family archive)*

García Navarro, Chief of Staff of the Division with *Comandante* Alemany just a few days before the latter's death. *(Juan Negreira archive)*

Above. Medals and documents belonging to *Coronel* García Navarro. *(Don Rodrigo foundation)*

Right. *Coronel* García Navarro harangues his audience of Blue Legion officers. Janedä (Estonia), March 1944.

Below. García Navarro, with the German Gold Cross hanging from his right pocket. Among those present are the Spanish Military Attaché in Berlin, Carlos Marín de Bernardo Lasheras (seated to the right of the photo, wearing glasses). *(Sáenz de Cabezón family archive)*

Antonio García Navarro was born in Pamplona on 18 November 1890. He fought in Morocco as an infantry officer in the 17th Borbón Infantry Regiment and in the Native Police between 1914 and 1917. While still belonging to the General Staff Corps (promotion, 1928) he led combat units during the Civil War, including the 61st Division which he commanded with the rank of lieutenant colonel. In the Russian campaign he served as Chief of Staff of the Blue Division, having arrived at the front in June 1943. In November he took command of the Blue Legion, a position he held until the unit was repatriated in April 1944. He went on to hold posts of increasing importance in the Spanish Army hierarchy, retiring with the honorary rank of lieutenant general. He died on 26 August 1985 in Madrid.

He is shown on page 34 wearing the uniform of a colonel (*oberst*) as commander of the Blue Legion towards the end of March 1944. Note the Spanish regulation belt he is wearing.

Comandante Pedro Merry Gordon, Victory Parade, Sevilla, 1952.

Comandante Enrique Herrera Marín, General Franco's Military Household; 1951.

Hauptmann Pedro Martínez de Tudela García, Commander of the 2nd Section *(bis)* of the General Staff; 1942.

JUNIOR OFFICERS

Over 2,200 Spanish officers fought in the Russian campaign. Maintaining the volunteers' morale and fighting capability in the field was the responsibility of the units' captains.

Pedro Merry Gordon was born in Jerez de la Frontera (Cadiz) on 21 May 1917. The uprising found him serving as an infantry cadet in Sevilla, whereupon he took part in securing the city under the orders of General Queipo de Llano. From 14 December 1936 he served in the 10th *Bandera* of the Legion being wounded on a number of occasions. He served in Russia as an infantry captain between April 1942 and October 1943 in the 9th Company of the 269th and as commander of what remained of the 2nd Battalion of the 269th after the battering it took at the Battle of Poselok. He also served in the 262nd (9th Company). He was wounded three times on 10 March 1943 at

Above and left. Two photographs of *Capitán de Infantería* Pedro Merry Gordon during his stay with the Blue Division. He is wearing his Medal of Suffering for the Motherland, earned in the Civil War. *(Merry Gordon family archive)*

Izhora, requiring a hospital stay of several months.

He retired with the rank of lieutenant general and died in Sevilla on 25 October 1993.

The illustration places Merry at a parade in the year 1952, wearing a Spanish regulation major's uniform and helmet. We can see very clearly his Infantry Assault

Merry, wearing his *General de la Legión* uniform, presides over a military ceremony in the 1960s, when he was *Capitán General* of the 2nd Military Region. *(Merry Gordon family archive)*

Badge (*Infanterie-Sturmabzeichen*), his Spanish War Cross for commanders, and his Iron Cross 1st Class. On the dress medal bar above we can see, albeit less clearly, his Red Cross of Military Merit (with various bars), his Iron Cross 2nd Class, and various campaign medals. Above there is a war merit promotion badge awarded in Russia between the end of January and 10 March 1943. Notice the five wound chevrons and a Collective Military Medal badge sewn onto his sleeve.

Pedro Martínez de Tudela García was born in Malaga on 12 August 1904. Born into a Civil Guard family, he joined the Civil Guard at the lowest rank and from there was rapidly promoted. He served in the African War and in the Civil War, being wounded six times. After his promotion to captain, he enlisted with the Blue Division in June 1941 and was posted to the 2nd Section of the General Staff, where he served as Head of the Internal Information Service (Staff Section II bis) until he was repatriated in February 1943. He continued in active service fighting against the Spanish *Maquis*. He died in Palma de Mallorca on 30 November 1992 with the honorary rank of brigadier of the Civil Guard.

Above. Martínez de Tudela standing next to a Blue Division NCO.

Left. Collective Military Medal.

Right. Military Merit Medal with red distinction, and 1936-39 Campaign Medal (right). These are some of the many medals earned by *Capitán* Martínez de Tudela.

Herrera Marín about to board a liaison aircraft (Junkers Ju 52) during his time in the Blue Legion. *(Herrera Marín family archive)*

He is shown on page 38 at the headquarters of the Blue Division. He is wearing the cords of the commander of the German Army patrol service, the ribbon of the Iron Cross 2nd Class (awarded in April 1942), and an impressive Spanish-type ribbon bar with ribbons mounted on strips of card in recognition of his courage in combat (Red Crosses, War Crosses, a Medal of Suffering for the Motherland, and others).

Once repatriated, like Tudela García, he also fought against the Spanish *Maquis* and took part in the Spanish mission in the Dominican Republic. He retired from the army in 1962 with the rank of lieutenant colonel. For many years he was the president of the *Hermandad Nacional de Alféreces Provisionales* (National Brotherhood of Acting Second-Lieutenants). He died in Madrid on 30 May 2000.

Left. On his return to Russia, after having been promoted to *Comandante*, he served in Franco's Military Household. This photo was taken during that period. *(Herrera Marín family archive).*

Below. *Capitán* Herrera Marín with *Alférez* Cavada at Ugolki, Volkhov, 9 July 1942. *(Herrera Marín family archive)*

Enrique Herrera Marín, born on 24 March 1919 in Tarragona, he abandoned his studies at the outbreak of the Civil War – he had passed the first year of Exact Sciences – and volunteered for service in the city of Melilla where he lived with his family.

The end of the war found him serving in the 11th *Bandera* of the Legion as an acting infantry captain. In the Blue Division and the Blue Legion (23 April 1942 to 20 April 1944) he served in the 2nd Battalion of the 269th for two years, as well as in other units.

Oberleutnant Fernando Martínez Cattáneo, 1st Battery, 250th Artillery Regiment; February 1942.

Alférez Adolfo de Montagut y de Martí, Returning from the Front; summer 1942.

Leutnant José Enrique Usunáriz Mocoroa, 11th Battery, 250th Artillery Regiment; September 1941.

He is shown during his time as adjutant to the commander-in-chief of Franco's Military Household, General Pablo Martín Alonso, in 1951. He is wearing his gala uniform and wears, among others, his medals won in combat, including the Silver Infantry Assault Badge (awarded 3 August 1943), the Iron Cross 1st Class (awarded 15 March 1944) and, above them, the German Close Combat Clasp (awarded 19 October 1943).

Fernando Martínez Cattáneo was born in Murcia on 30 May 1917. In July 1936, while in his second year of engineering, he joined the Falange militia in Oviedo and was wounded in action in October of that year. As a provisional artillery officer, he fought at Brunete and on other fronts. In July 1941, he completed his studies at the

Above. Teniente Martínez Cattáneo is posing in front of a 105mm artillery piece belonging to his battery. *(Martínez-Cattáneo family archive)*

Left. Teniente Martínez Cattáneo's funeral at Podberesje. *(Martínez-Cattáneo family archive)*

School of Agricultural Engineers in Madrid where he was a Spanish Students' Union (hereinafter SEU) representative, before he joined the Blue Division. He was assigned to the 1st Battery of the 250th Regiment in which he won the Iron Cross 2nd Class posthumously after taking a direct hit from a Soviet grenade on 4 April 1942. He was buried in Podberesje before his remains were repatriated and reburied in the Blue Division's tomb in La Almudena cemetery in Madrid on 4 December 2003.

A portrait photo of Alférez Usunáriz heading for the frontline. *(Usunáriz Mocoroa family archive)*

He is shown on page 42 in front of one his artillery pieces, talking on the phone to his fire control post during the fighting in autumn 1941.

José Enrique Usunáriz Mocoroa was born in San Sebastián on 29 March 1921. He spent the first part of the Civil War in the ancillary services due to his young age, until he was old enough to serve at the front in the 14th Light Artillery Regiment. By the end of the war he had risen to the rank of provisional second lieutenant in the artillery, the rank with which he joined the Blue Division. He served in the 11th Battery in the 4th Heavy Artillery Group. While at the Novgorod front he received orders to report to the Artillery Academy in Spain, leaving the front on 25 November 1941. His brother Joaquín María, an

Below. Comandante Castro Escudero (second on the right), commander of the IV Group of the 250th Artillery Regiment, relaxing with a number of Spanish officers, among whom we can see Usunáriz, first from the left. *(Usunáriz Mocoroa family archive)*

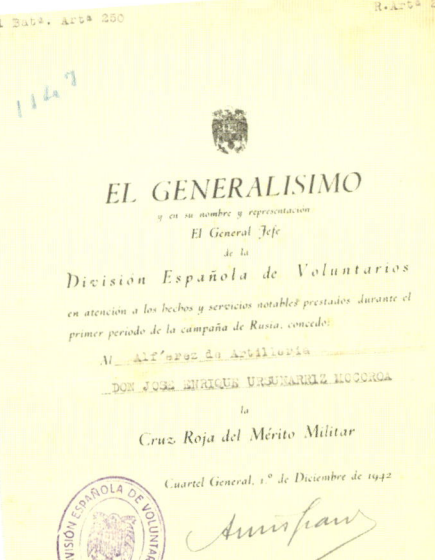

Right. The citation awarding a Military Medal Red Cross to Usunáriz for his service in Russia. *(Usunáriz Mocoroa family archive)*

Left and above. Two photos of Alférez De Montagut on the Russian Front. *(De Montagut family archive)*

a German artillery second lieutenant's uniform with a Spanish ribbon bar.

Adolfo de Montagut y de Martí was born on 30 October 1918 in Barcelona, the same city that the outbreak of the Civil War found him in. He escaped to the Nationalist Zone in the winter of 1937, and fought at Teruel and on the Ebro front with the 5th Battalion of the 23rd América Infantry Regiment, finishing the war with the rank of provisional second lieutenant. With this rank he joined the Blue Division from the 16th Infantry Regiment in Lérida. He initially served with the 12th Company of the 263rd and, during the march to the front, in September 1941, he was promoted to adjutant under Lieutenant Colonel Canillas. He left the Army in 1945 to join the reserve as lieutenant. In civilian life he worked in the construction business, dying in Barcelona on 16 June 1998.

He is shown here having returned from the Russian front in the summer of 1942. He is wearing a Spanish uniform with the ribbon of the Iron Cross 2nd Class correctly looped through the second button hole (awarded on 8 April 1942).

Above. Three officers of the 263rd Infantry Regiment.

artillery lieutenant, was also in Russia. José Enrique continued in the Army, retiring as a brigadier. He died in Valladolid on February 13, 2011.

He appears on page 42 in a studio pose in September 1941 during a stop in Grodno on his way to the front. He is wearing

Feldwebel José Cogollos Vicens, Riga Hospital; September 1943.

Feldwebel Eleuterio Pertierra del Busto, 250th Transport Group; September 1941.

Feldwebel Tomás García Fernández, *Feldgendarmerie*; November 1942.

NCOs

Around 4,500 NCOs served with the Blue Division, including Civil Guards acting as NCOs. They played a decisive role in the day-to-day running of the Blue Division and were instrumental in its military success.

José Cogollos Vicens was born in Valencia on August 7, 1916. He was enlisted by the Republican Army as a medic – he had previously been a medical student – but after many adventures he deserted to the Nationalist side and spent the rest of the war in armoured units. He joined the Valencia militia in March 1942, serving in the Medical Group in various hospitals, including Grigorowo and Riga. Later, with the rank of warrant officer and, later still, provisional second lieutenant (medical), he served

Two divisionarios *at Riga, dressed in the white tunic of the summer uniform worn by the Wehrmacht. It is highly unusual to find a photo such as this, since very few Spaniards wore this outfit. (Esteban-Infantes family archive)*

in the Sapper Battalion and the 2nd Battalion of the 269th Regiment, respectively. He married a Latvian and returned to Spain to work as a doctor for the railway company Renfe and in Sidi Ifni, Morocco. He died in Valencia in 1987.

In the illustration he wears the uniform of a medical sergeant (*Feldwebel*) in Riga, around the month of September 1943, convalescing from a wound in the right leg received on 23 July 1943. He is wearing the white summer uniform of the *Wehrmacht*, with epaulettes showing his rank and medical badge. On the German-style ribbon bar

Another sergeant, Daniel Martínez Martínez, who like Cogollos served in the 250th Medical Group. On his breast he wears the ribbon of the Russian Front Medal awarded to those who fought in the first winter campaign (also humorously referred to by the troops as the Frozen Meat Medal).

Two portrait photos of Cogollos Vicens during the Russian Campaign. *(Cogollos Vicens family archive)*

he wears the German War Merit Cross 2nd Class (KVK2) with Swords, and the Iron Cross 2nd Class. He is also wearing the Iron Cross 1st Class, although there is no official record of his having been awarded it.

Tomás García Fernández was born in Valdecastillo (León) on August 19, 1916. After fighting in the Civil War as an artilleryman, he joined the Civil Guard in September 1940. He took part in the Russian campaign from the year 1942, forming part of the rearguard police service of the Blue Division. He returned to Spain on 4 September 1943 and left the Civil Guard voluntarily in August 1944. After that we lose track of him.

He is shown on page 46 in the uniform of a *Feldgendarme* traffic policeman on the Russian front.

Eleuterio Pertierra del Busto was born in Cudillero (Asturias) on 8 August 1917. He took part in the defence of Oviedo and ended the Civil War as sergeant in the depot company of the 8th Sappers-Miners Battalion attached to the 108th Division. He enlisted in the Blue Division in July 1941, serving in the Transport Group until September 1942. His brother Gerardo was also in the Blue Division, with the Quartermaster Corps. In 1953 he retired from

Above. A Spanish Civil Guard performing control duties control on the Russian Front. *(Crescencio Burón family archive)*

Right. Tomás García Fernández, a Civil Guard with the Blue Division. Note the Falangist badge on his left breast pocket. *(Núñez Calvo archive)*

the army reserve as engineer captain to set up a footwear store, which he ran until he reached retirement age. He died in Gijón on 4 July 2008.

He is depicted pn page 46 as a sergeant of the Transport Group in the autumn of 1941. We can see the sky blue piping on his cap and epaulettes identifying him as a member of the Transport Group. The only clues identifying him as Spanish are his arm badge and his Falangist yoke and arrows.

Luis Nieto García, born in Medina del Campo (Valladolid) in 1917 and a member of the *FE de las JONS*, he was at the La Montaña barracks in Madrid on July 20, 1936 when the Civil War broke out. He spent the war in Las Ventas prison. As a sergeant in the *FET y de las JONS* militia in Russia (3rd company of the 269th) he became a living legend for his acts of heroism. Once the campaign was over, he worked in Ponferrada as a chemical engineer and became the city's mayor between 1957 and 1962. He was also a member of the National Council of the Movement and President of the *Hermandad de la*

Above, centre and left. Eleuterio Pertierra del Busto. Military Medal Red Cross and various photos of this sergeant of the Blue Division Transport Group. *(Pertierra del Busto family archive and collection)*

Unteroffizier Luis Nieto García, 3rd Company, 269th Infantry Regiment; December 1941.

Sargento Francisco Grau Pérez, 132nd Command of the Civil Guard, 1952.

Sargento Maximino Pérez Pérez, In Madrid on returning from the Russian Front; May 1942.

PABLO SAGARRA - ÓSCAR GONZÁLEZ - LUCAS MOLINA

División Azul (Brotherhood of the Blue Division) for many years.

He was named Adoptive Son of Ponferrada in the month of September 1968. He died in Madrid on February 11, 1998.

We see him standing to attention at Colonel Martínez Esparza's command post in Schevelevo during the visit that General Moscardó made on the morning

Above. Luis Nieto at Schevelevo, during General Moscardó's historic visit to the Blue Division. *(FDA archive)*

Left. Luis Nieto at the celebration of the 50th anniversary of the arrival at the front of the Blue Division. He is wearing a blue Falangist shirt and the medals he won in the Civil War and on the Russian Campaign.

of December 3, 1941. He is carrying combat gear and wearing a blue Falangist shirt and the ribbon of his recently awarded Iron Cross 2nd Class.

Francisco Grau Pérez was born in Polop de la Marina (Alicante) on 18 June 1915. Like his father before him he was a Civil Guard, and July 1936 found him stationed at Cherta (Tarragona). He served in the

The Civil Guard Grau Pérez at Novgorod during his posting at Division Headquarters. *(Grau Pérez family archive)*

Republican Army until he could cross over to the Nationalist Zone at Belchite on 2 January 1937. He spent the rest of the war performing security duties on various fronts. In the Blue Division he served at the divisional headquarters with the 4th Section of the General Staff (Services), although for two days he did actually fight on the front line. In peace time he remained in the Civil Guard and retired as a major. He died in Benidorm on 14 October 2006.

He appears in dress uniform in the early 1950s, when he was a sergeant in the 132nd Command of the Civil Guard in Lérida. Apart from his war medals he is wearing a Spanish-made Iron Cross, purely decorative as he was not awarded any such medal in Russia.

Maximino Pérez was born in Fuenlabrada (Madrid) on February 27, 1912. He was the head of the local *FE de las JONS* but after the outbreak of the Civil War he managed to keep a low profile until his village was liberated by the Nationalists on 2 November

Above. On his wedding day *Sargento* Grau wears his medals earned in the Civil War and on the Russian Front. *(Grau Pérez family archive)*

Right. *Comandante* Grau at his home in Benidorm after retiring from the army. *(Grau Pérez family archive)*

A beautiful photo taken in Madrid on the morning of May 27, 1942, of *Sargento* Maximino Pérez on his return from the Russian Front. *(FDA archive)*

1936. He immediately entered into combat, first in the 2nd *Bandera Falange de Castilla* and later in the 1st Battalion of the 2nd Tank Group of the Spanish Legion. He belonged to the first contingent of the Blue Division, serving with the 2nd Company of the Anti-Tank Group. On his return to Spain, as commander of the 1st *Centuria*[1] of Franco's Guard he worked as a truck driver and as a bodyguard for government ministers Solís and Arrase. He died in Madrid on 21 January 1961.

He is shown on page 50 in Madrid, on 27 May 1942, in the Retiro Park as standard

Individual Military Medal and *Wehrmacht* Eagle belonging to Maximino Pérez. *(Pérez Pérez family collection)*

bearer of the 1st Repatriation Battalion of the Blue Division. He is wearing the uniform of an infantry sergeant, with a badge showing him to be a Falangist and wearing his three most important medals; the Iron Crosses earned in Russia (awarded on January 9 and April 18, 1942 respectively), and the Individual Military Medal won in the Civil War on May 13, 1938, on Hill 1597 of the El Pobo sector (Teruel), driving a *negrillo* Panzer I tank.

Maximino Pérez with his wife, María Montero Montero. He is wearing the uniform of the Movement, on which can be seen his Individual Military Medal and Iron Cross 1st Class, the latter won on the Russian Front. *(Pérez Pérez family archive)*

---

1   A *Centuria* was a third of a *Tercio*.

Gefreiter Antonio Ponte Anido, 3rd Company, 250th Sappers Battalion; February 1943.

Schütze Ángel Aybar Redondo, Skiers Company; January 1942.

Unteroffizier Juan Sandoval Caballero, 3rd Company, 250th Anti-Tank Group; summer 1943.

NCOs AND MEN

Ángel Aybar Redondo was born in Madrid on 18 July 1926. When he was just fifteen years old, still a high school student, he enlisted in the Blue Division by lying about his age. In November 1941, while in the 2nd Radio Company, he was chosen to form part of the Ski Company of the 250th (he had some skiing skills that he had learned as a member of the Mountaineer *Centuria* of the SEU). He took part in the heroic Lake Ilmen crossing as a runner for Lieutenant Otero de Arce and was one of the few uninjured survivors of the operation. He was awarded the Iron Cross 2nd

Above. Spanish skiers of the Blue Division. *(FDA archive)*

Left. Angel Aybar (right), wearing his Iron Cross, strolling with Alberto Lamamié de Clairac when both formed part of the *Centuria de Montañeros.*

Right. A portrait photo of Aybar during his service with the Blue Division.

Class, the Infantry Assault Badge, and the Collective Military Medal. He went on to study engineering at the ICAI School of Engineering and worked for Madrid City Council until he retired. He died in the capital of Spain on 3 May 2010.

German soldiers on the Russian Front wearing winter clothing.

He is shown on page 54 on the frontline in the first winter of 1941-42. He is protected by a white anorak and trousers, the usual garb of a Ski Company soldier, and is carrying combat gear, including a flare pistol in his right hand.

Juan Sandoval Caballero was born on 25 November 1921 in Cieza (Murcia). He spent the Civil War as a teenager in the town of his birth before joining the Blue Division in March 1942. He served as a shorthand typist soldier in the 4th Section of the General Staff and in the month of August 1942 he was transferred to the Anti-Tank Group (3rd Company) where he was wounded in December of that year. He remained in this unit until the end of the campaign, being promoted to corporal and then to sergeant by battlefield promotion. On his return from Russia he ran a bar, was a clerk in the Spanish Trade Union Organization, and

Right. Cruz de Guerra *awarded to Sandoval in Russia. (Sandoval Caballero family collection)*

Below. Anti-tank troops posing on a light 37 mm Pak 35/36 gun of the Blue Division. *(FDA archive)*

Above. Sandoval, anti-tank sergeant in the Blue Division. *(Sandoval Caballero family archive)*

councillor for the town of Cieza. He died in Cieza on 28 July 2010.

Juan is depicted on page 54 as a sergeant, in the role of gun commander, during his service in the Anti-Tank Group in the summer of 1943. He is wearing the ribbons of the German War Merit Cross (KVK2) and the Iron Cross 2nd Class (the latter awarded on April 20, 1943), and the Wound Badge.

Left. State-of-the-art anti-tank materiel used by the Division in 1943, among which we can see three types of mines: two Tellermine T mines and a magnetic type-H mine at the bottom left of the photo. The latter was used by assault sappers. *(Ortega Gil family archive)*

Below. The hero Ponte Anido in one of the very few photos of him that have survived. *(Ponte Anido family archive)*

Antonio Ponte Anido was born in Ponte do Porco (La Coruña) on October 8, 1920. After being mobilized at the age of eighteen, he took part in the Catalonia offensive in 1938-1939 with the 3rd *Bandera* of *FET y de las JONS*. He belonged to the 2nd Battalion of the 8th Mixed Engineer Regiment of the 81st Division before he joined the Blue Division, in which served in the 3rd Company of the Sapper Battalion during the campaign of the first winter. After a period of convalescence at the hospital in Königsberg he refused to be sent back to Spain and was promoted to sapper corporal. On 10 February 1943, he died during the Battle of Krasny Bor, when he single-handedly placed an AT mine between the track and the drivetrain of an enemy tank.

This hero, who was posthumously awarded the Laureate Cross of Saint Ferdinand, is shown on page 54 just before the Battle of Krasny-Bor, carrying a grenade and an anti-tank mine, wearing the uniform of the second winter of the campaign.

Above. Postcard sent by sapper Ponte Anido to his family just before he died in Russia. *(Ponte Anido family collection)*

Right. Sappers on exercise in Russia. *(Juan Negreira archive)*

Schutze Jaime Dolado Gonzalo, Königsberg Hospital; Summer 1943.

Volunteer Gregorio Pozo Crespo, 27th Marching Battalion; September 1943.

Schutze Manuel Guijarro Agero, in Germany on his way back to Spain; July 1942.

Above. Medals belonging to the *divisionario* Hernández Ramos. *(Hernández Ramos collection)*

Right. Santiago Hernández Ramos, foot soldier in the Division. *(Santiago Hernández archive)*

Montoya is seen on page 62 in combat gear in a trench on the Leningrad front in the spring 1943. He is wearing a camouflage poncho and handling an MG 34 machine gun.

Santiago Hernández Ramos was born on March 26, 1924 in León. He lived in Madrid during the Civil War, joining the Falangist Youth Organization at the end of it. As leader of the *Centuria Leones de Castilla* he joined the Blue Division, serving in the 5th Company of the 2nd Battalion of the 269th. He was wounded in action at Kotovsky on 24 August 1942 and was repatriated

Left. Medal of Suffering for the Motherland awarded to this divisionario for the wound he received on 24 August 1942.

Right. The veteran Hernández Ramos in a recent Day of the Hispanic World parade in Madrid.

PABLO SAGARRA - ÓSCAR GONZÁLEZ - LUCAS MOLINA

30 August 1943. Khaki trousers, jackboots, and a blue shirt on which can be seen the hand-embroidered Blue Division shield and the swan insignia identifying him as a member of one of the new OOJJ (Youth Organizations), which he joined in Ciudad Real in April 1939.

Alfredo Montoya Crespo, born in Santurde de Rioja (La Rioja) on 27 February 1920, was mobilized during the Civil War, joining the army in May 1938. He served in a *Tabor* of the 1st *Tetuan* Regular Forces Group, with which he fought and was wounded at the Battle of the Ebro. Once recovered from his wounds he was involved in clean-up operations against Republicans hiding out in Asturias after the war had ended. While in Ibiza with his *tabor* in the spring of 1942 he joined the Blue Division and was sent to the 12th Machine Gun Company of the 262nd Regiment. He fought on the Volkhov and Leningrad

Above. Montoya on the beach at Dibulti, Riga. *(Montoya family archive)*

Left. An MG 34 machine-gun post on the Russian Front. It was a fabulous weapon and the divisionarios made great use of it. *(FDA archive)*

fronts until he was repatriated in October 1943. Back in Spain he finally graduated from university and returned to his home village where he worked in subsistence farming. When his wife passed away he went to live in Trápaga (Vizcaya) where he died on 18 January 2011.

Schutze Alfredo Montoya Crespo, 12th Company, 262nd Infantry Regiment; summer, 1943.

Schutze Santiago Hernández Ramos, 5th Company, 269th Infantry Regiment, April 1942.

Soldado Emilio Sáinz de Varanda Moreno, prisoner in the USSR, onboard the *Semiramis*. Barcelona 1954.

Gregorio Pozo Crespo in Logroño, the day he left for the Russian Front. *(Pozo family archive)*

Private Dolado is a classic type among the Spanish troops. He is depicted on page 58 in Königsberg during the spring-summer of 1943 and, although he is wearing a private's tunic and belt, he has taken the liberty of kitting himself out with some officer's boots. He is proudly wearing various Falangist badges and the shield of the SEU.

Gregorio Pozo Crespo was born in Ciudad Real on 28 November 1923. A member of the Falangist Youth Front, he joined the Blue Division in Valencia, forming part of the last marching battalion, the 27th, which left Logroño on 30 September 1943. He joined the 9th Company of the 263rd Regiment stationed in the Volosovo area and stayed on in the Blue Legion (6th Company, 2nd *Bandera*) as a rifleman, taking part in various engagements, until he was repatriated in April 1944. He worked for a long time for the *Banco*

Left. An ID card photo of Gregorio Pozo. *(Pozo family archive)*

Below. Souvenir of the Blue Division brought back from Russia by Gregorio Pozo. *(Pozo family archive)*

Exterior de España, and served as mayor of El Aaiún (Spanish Sahara) and as a parliamentary representative in the 1960s. He died in Madrid on 5 August 2013.

Pozo is wearing the uniform in which he left Logroño bound for Germany on

The *divisionario* Pozo at his home in Madrid, a few months before his death.

The volunteer Jame Dolado wearing a German uniform. He was a founder member of the SEU, as certified by the attached document. *(Retógenes Association collection)*

Jaime Dolado Gonzalo was born in Sigüenza (Guadalajara) on 30 December 1923. After moving to Madrid with his family, on 20 October 1935, while attending the prestigious school, Instituto Cardenal Cisneros, he became a member of the SEU and joined the *Centuria de Balillas*. The outbreak of the Civil War found him on holiday in the Nationalist Zone and he spent the war between Soria and Navarra (where he had relatives) collaborating

Right. Seville, 24 May 1952. *Teniente Interventor* Jaime Dolado's wedding on his return from Russia, after having attended Faculty of Law and the *Academia de Intervención* military academy. *(Retógenes Association archive)*

Below. Emblem of the SEU and medals won in Russia by Jaime Dolado. *(Retógenes Association collection)*

with the second-line Falange. On finishing his high-school studies he tried to enlist in the Blue Division but was turned down due to being too young in June 1941. He tried again in February 1942, this time successfully. In Russia he fought on the Volkhov front with the 5th Company of the 263rd before being sent to the rear with malaria in August 1942. He convalesced in Königsberg and once given the all-clear he remained there serving in the hospital's medical detachment until it was time for his repatriation in October 1943. On his return to Spain he graduated in Economics and joined the Military Intervention Corps, in which he reached the rank of major. He died in Sevilla on 11 April 1965.

MEN

Left. Manuel Guijarro Agero, Blue Division volunteer. *(Guijarro family archive)*

Manuel Guijarro Agero was born in Madrid on 9 June 1921 and joined the Zaragoza Falange when he was just fifteen years old, serving on the Villamayor de Gállego front until he was discharged for being underage. He enlisted in the Blue Division in June 1941, serving in the 3rd Company of the 262nd (81mm mortar section). He fought at the bridgehead and was a casualty from frostbite in both feet; he spent nearly two months in hospital before returning to the front in February 1942. He remained in Russia until July of that year when he was repatriated. He went on to work as a journalist and joined the Intervention Corps, in which he retired with the rank of colonel. He died in Madrid on 3 May 1994.

Pennant of the SEU, the organization to which Guijarro belonged when he set off for the Russian Front. (Retógenes Association collection)

Guijarro (right) with two fellow soldiers having a beer. *(Guijarro family archive)*

Manual Guijarro, a dyed-in-the-wool Falangist, is shown having returned from the front in July 1942. He is wearing a *feldbluse* (field tunic) with the collar of his blue shirt worn outside, as was the custom. Note how he has removed some of the badges from his uniform before returning it to the German quartermaster in order to take them back to Spain as souvenirs. The German *Wehrmacht* eagle has gone from the above the right breast pocket, as has the Spanish badge on the sleeve on the same side. Contrary to custom he is wearing an SEU badge on his left breast pocket, where Falangists usually sewed the yoke and arrows, and not on the right pocket.

Above, below and right. Three moving photos of the repatriation of Emilio Sáinz de Varanda in 1954 after he spent eleven years in a Gulag. *(Sáinz de Varanda archive)*

to complete his convalescence in Madrid. There he worked as a civil servant in a ministry until he retired in 1984. He belongs to the *Hermandad de la División Azul* (Brotherhood of the Blue Division) and lives in Madrid.

He is depicted on page 62 on the front line, at the Volkhov Pocket around the month of April 1942. His Walther P38 is unholstered.

Emilio Sáinz de Varanda Moreno was born in Santa Cruz de Bezana (Cantabria) on 12 May 1922. At the start of the Civil War he was living in the city of Santander until he was bombed out of his home. He and his family moved to Bezana until the Nationalist troops arrived. In April 1942 he signed up for the Blue Division and served in the campaign in the Staff Company of the Anti-Tank Group. He was wounded in the Battle of Krasny-Bor on 11 February 1943, captured by the Russians, and sent to work at the Gulag labour camps at Makarino, Karaganda and Borovichi among others. After his repatriation he worked in the welfare department of the Santander Provincial

Sáinz de Varanda's ex-POW ID card.

Schutze José Miguel Guitarte Yrigaray, Assault Section, 262nd Infantry Regiment; April 1942.

Schutze Dionisio Ridruejo Jiménez, 2nd Company, Anti-Tank Group; October 1941.

Schutze Luis Aguilar Sanabria, Radio Company, 250th Signals Battalion; May 1942.

Government until he retired. He was widowed on 27 September 2011 and continues to live in Santander.

Emilio is shown on page 62 leaning against the rail of the *Semiramis* on 2 April 1954, as the ship approaches the Port of Barcelona to make landfall in Spain. His physical appearance tells of the hardships suffered in the Russian prison camps. There is nothing left of his Wehrmacht uniform after eleven years in the Gulag; he is wearing a Russian *telegreika*, cap and trousers.

José Miguel Guitarte Yrigaray, born in 1915, was a communist activist studying medicine at the Central University of Madrid when he met and befriended Agustín Aznar, a prominent Falangist activist, in 1933, after which he became a staunch Falangist. He was a national triumvir of the SEU and became its General Secretary in October 1934. He was arrested before the Nationalist rebellion and spent the war in prison in Madrid. In August 1939, he was made national head of the SEU and while still holding that position he joined the Blue Division. He fought as a simple foot soldier in the 262nd Regiment, Assault Section, at the position on the Volkhov front known as *El Alcázar*, among other sectors. He was repatriated in July 1942 and appointed Member of Parliament (*Procurador en Cortes*), but held the post only briefly. He died in Madrid on 21 November 1943 at the age of just twenty-eight.

Centre. Guitarte, National Head of the SEU, wearing a German uniform while serving with the Blue Division.

Below. Guitarte inspecting a Soviet four-barrel anti-aircraft machine gun captured by the Germans during Operation *Barbarossa.*

Above. Guitarte with the uniform of the Movement on his trip to Italy in 1942. (Gutiérrez del Castillo archive)

Bujeiro portrays Guitarte at Dresden, on page 66, on April 19, 1942, during the Congress of European Students and Combatants. His uniform bears the ribbon of the KVK2 (but not the Iron Cross 2nd Class since he would not be awarded that distinction until a few days later on 27 April) and on his left sleeve we can see the coveted Silver Palm of the Falange, awarded on 18 June 1935.

Luis Aguilar Sanabria was born in Madrid on 3 March 1908. A long serving *camisa vieja* (old shirt) Falangist – he had belonged to the Falange since 1 February 1934 – he was arrested in April 1936 and sent to prison in Huelva. After the uprising he was released and fought in the Civil War on the Madrid front as the head of a Falangist *Centuria* while also working alongside the Spanish Youth Organization in Sevilla. In the Blue Division he served in the Radio Company of the Signals Battalion until his repatriation in July 1942. In peacetime he worked as an industrial technical engineer and served as a Member of Parliament (*Procurador en Cortes*) in Franco's government. He died

Above and below. Aguilar Sanabria during his pilgrimage to the Santuario del Pilar in gratitude for his safe return from the Russian Front. *(Aguilar family archive)*

Above. *Wehrmacht* signals troops. Their work during the war was vital.

Left. The Falangist *Dionisio* Ridruejo, a volunteer in the 2nd Company of the Anti-Tank Group of the Division.

Above. Spanish *divisionarios* of the 2nd Company of the Anti-Tank Group, in which Ridruejo served.

Below. Ridruejo as National Head of Press and Propaganda. His political ideas were later to evolve radically; he became a social-democrat who openly opposed Franco's regime which he had previously served.

in Toba de Valdivielso (Madrid), his wife's home village, on 3 August 1979.

He is shown in the illustration operating a portable HF transmitter-receiver (a TornFu b1). On his Spanish ribbon bar he displays his Civil War decorations, and wears two other insignias; one is the yoke and arrows and the other is the badge of the Hitler Youth Organization, which he knew well from the visit he made to Germany in 1938.

Dionisio Ridruejo Jiménez was born in Burgo de Osma (Soria) in 1912. He joined the Falange Española in 1933 and during the war was appointed head of the National Press and Propaganda Agency. After being sacked from this position in May 1941 he left for Russia to serve in the 2nd Company of the Anti-Tank Group, fighting at Possad among other places. Once back in Spain he became an opponent of Franco, firstly for not handing all the power over to the Falange and later, from a more social-democratic stance, because of Franco's authoritarianism. This led to his suffering a number of periods of arrest and prison. He was a renowned author and poet who travelled widely. He died in Madrid on 29 June 1975.

He is depicted on page 66 as an anti-tank soldier on the Volkhov front (autumn 1941), with his blue shirt buttoned up under his German uniform tunic.

Hauptmann Urbano Gómez García, Headquarters Company Commander, Blue Legion; April 1944.

Schutze Gustavo Prado Fernández, Headquarters Company of the 2nd Bandera, Blue Legion; January 1944.

Oberleutnant Konstantin Goguijonachvili, Interpreter, Blue Legion; February 1944.

BLUE LEGION

Between November 1943 and April 1944, the month when the unit was finally repatriated, the successor of the Blue Division, known as the Blue Legion, continued the fight against Communism, then at just regimental strength.

Urbano Gómez García, was born in Villasecino (León) on 2 June 1913, and joined the Falange Española before the war. July 18 found him in his native village. From there he was able to reach Nationalist Zone and join in the fighting. He fought with various Falangist units: the 13th *Centuria* of *FE de las JONS*, the 1st *Bandera de Castilla*, and the 3rd *Bandera* of *FET y de las JONS*. At the end of the war he was serving in the 1st *Tercio* of the Legion as a provisional lieutenant. Having held the rank of temporary captain since the autumn of 1942, on the Russian campaign he commanded first the 11th and then the 1st companies of the 263rd Regiment. At the head of this latter unit he personally destroyed two Russian tanks at the Battle of Krasny-Bor, during which action he was seriously wounded. Once recovered he returned to the front before joining the Blue Legion as adjutant to *Coronel* García Navarro. He arrived back in Spain in May 1944. Urbano Gómez retired with the rank of army colonel to go into the farming business. He died in Madrid on November 29, 1996.

He is shown in the uniform of a captain on the Staff of the Blue Legion. As well as the medals and ribbons awarded for his acts of heroism in combat the previous year (Iron Crosses plus Tank Destruction, Infantry Assault and Black Wound badges), he also wears the badge of the Spanish Legion over his left breast pocket.

Left. A studio portrait of *Capitán* Urbano Gómez. Note the badge of the Legion in which he had served while in Spain.
(Gómez García family archive)

Below. From left to right, *Teniente* Vega Viguera, *Comandante* Abenia Arenas, and *Capitán* Gómez García, all serving in the Blue Division.
(Gómez García family archive)

Teniente Goguijonachvili in the Tercio de Navarra during the Spanish Civil War. (Emilio Herrera archive)

Konstantin Goguijonachvili was born in Georgia, served as a cavalry officer in the Tsar's army in the First World War and later in the White Army during the Russian Civil War (1918-1921). In the Spanish Civil War, he served in the Legion and then in the Carlist militia known as the *Requeté*, specifically in the *Tercio de Navarra*, in which he fought courageously as a lieutenant. He was wounded when the Asturian front was breached in September 1937, losing the sight in one eye. He served with distinction in several operations, including the battle for the Talavera de la Reina bridgehead on 27 March 1938. While living in Madrid, at the age of 50 he joined the Blue Division in June 1941. He acted as an interpreter for the 269th Regiment, the 250th Reserve Battalion, and in the Blue Legion. His age did not prevent him from distinguishing himself in a number of actions, in one of which he destroyed a Russian tank. He became an honorary second as a lieutenant. He was given Spanish nationality, and worked for a time in the Commission of Military History. It is not known when he died.

He is pictured on pages 70 to 71 in Jäneda (Estonia) in February 1944. He is wearing a Spanish ribbon bar with several Spanish, German and Russian decorations, along with a number of decorations and badges earned with the Blue Division.

Above. Equipment and badges carried by Blue Legion troops. (Manuel Pérez Rubio collection)

Below. Officers of the Staff of the Blue Legion. To the left is Teniente Goguijonachvili. (Retógenes Association archive)

Left. Machine-gun troops of the Blue Legion listen attentively to General Priess, commander of the 121st Division of the *Wehrmacht.* Among other officers we see *Teniente Coronel* Modesto Sáenz de Cabezón (with overcoat and visor cap), *Oberst* Knüppel (to his left, wearing a peaked cap), General Priess and *Coronel* García Navarro (to the far right of the photo). Behind García Navarro we can just see Prince Metternich's head. *(Sáenz de Cabezón family archive)*

Gustavo Prado Fernández was born on 12 November 1923 in Laviana (Asturias). He spent the Civil War as a teenager in his home village before joining the Oviedo militia in July 1942. He left Spain bound for Russia with the 19th Marching Battalion, arriving at the front in January 1943, where he served in the 15th Company of the 263rd. When the Blue Division was disbanded he stayed behind in the Blue Legion serving in the Headquarter Company of the 2nd *Bandera*, before being finally repatriated on 11 April 1944. He received several decorations for his service in Russia, including the silver Infantry Assault badge. After a time working as a mechanic he worked on the railways until he reached retirement age. He died in his native town on 27 January 2014.

Above and below left. Volunteer Gustavo Prado in the Blue Division, photographed in June 1942 and again at his home in Asturias just months before he passed away *(Prado Fernández archive)*

Schutze Jorge Mayoral Mora, 102nd Company, 357th Infantry Division; February 1945.

SS-Untersturmführer Ricardo Botet Moro, 3rd Company II/70th SS Regiment, Wallonien Division; March 1945.

SS-Obersturmführer Lorenzo Ocañas Serrano, Ezquerra Unit; April 1945.

LAST VOLUNTEERS

Jorge Mayoral Mora, was born on 4 August 1922, in Don Benito (Badajoz). In the Civil War his elder brother José was trained in the URSS and fought as a Tupolev *Katiuska* bomber pilot before being killed in action on 7 February 1938, during the Battle of Alfambra (Teruel). He was apparently shot down by the German pilot, Wilhelm Balthasar. Meanwhile Jorge, a staunch Falange member, enlisted in the first contingent of *divisionarios* and was sent to the Veterinary Company. In 1942 he was sent home but he joined up again in June 1943, this time serving in the machine-gun company of the 1st Battalion[1] of the 263rd and later in the Blue Legion. In June 1944, he secretly joined the battalion of Spanish volunteers known as the Ghost Battalion at the training camp at Hall in Tirol (Austria). From February 1945 he fought in the Spanish 102nd Company, part of the German 357th Infantry Division. He was taken prisoner in Czechoslovakia on the following 23 March and spent nine years in a Soviet gulag. He finally returned to Spain on board the *Semiramis* on 2 April 1954 and established his residence in Madrid, where he died on 17 April 2013.

In the illustration we see him as a platoon leader corporal wearing a German Army uniform in the winter 1944-45 at the training camp at Hall in Tirol. Certain details show his nationality, his length of service in the fight against Communism, and his ideological convictions.

Centre. A POW photo of Mayoral Mora taken by the NKVD during his imprisonment in a Gulag. (Boris Kovalev archive)

Right. A photo of Mayoral Mora, retired from the INP.

Left. Mayoral Mora, third from the left in the top row, on board the *Semiramis*.

---

1 Other sources have him in the 4th Battalion [ed.]

Botet Moro in civvies in 1946, shortly before his repatriation.

Ricardo Botet Moro was born in Barcelona on 24 December 1921, to a Spanish father and a mother of German descent. He joined the Blue Division in Madrid in June 1941. For the first year of the campaign he served in the 2nd Battalion of the 269th as an interpreter (he spoke both German and French). After returning briefly to Spain he re-enlisted in 1943 in the Blue Legion before joining the 28th *Wallonien* Division in the summer of 1944. He served in the 3rd Company of the 2nd Battalion of the SS/70th Regiment, a unit in which he was not the only Spaniard (he also met León Degrelle, the founder of the Rexist party, there). He fought at Stargard and Stettin and in April 1945 he joined the *Ezquerra* Unit of the Waffen SS, an unattached company under the command of the Falangist Miguel Ezquerra. He also fought at the Battle of Berlin during which he managed to break out and escape to the Allied Zone where he was taken prisoner by the British. After serving some time in a British prison camp he was sent back to Spain in 1946. He worked in the hospitality business until he died in Malaga on 18 July 2008.

He is shown on page 74 as a *SS-Untersturmführer* (second lieutenant) during his time in the *Wallonien* Division, around about the month of March 1945. He is carrying a *Panzerfaust* anti-tank weapon and wears

Above. Botet during his time in the Blue Legion.

Right. Sargento Botet at the Leningrad Front. His blue shirt collar worn outside his *Wehrmacht* tunic shows that he is a good Falangist.

The first from the left is Alférez Ocañas Serrano, posing with three officers of his unit, the 2nd Company of the 263rd Regiment, in October 1941. On the far right is Alférez Ángel Ruiz Ayúcar. *(Ruiz Ayúcar family archive)*

the decorations won in the two periods in which he fought against the Soviets.

Lorenzo Ocañas Serrano, born in Montoro, Cordoba, on 11 April 1915, fought in the Civil War from 5 August 1936, with the *Tercio de Requetés Virgen de los Reyes*, as a machine-gun feeder. On 1 July 1941, he joined the Blue Division in Castellón de la Plana with the rank of second lieutenant. He served in the 2nd Company of the 263rd and was lightly wounded in the fighting at Possad on 4 December 1941. Early in August 1944 he secretly crossed the border and reported for duty at Innsbruck (Austria) where most of the Spanish volunteers had been assembled. In November, he took command of a section in the 3rd Company of the *Wallonien* Division and, after the battle of Pomerania, in February 1945, he joined the *Ezquerra* Unit. He took part in the defence of Berlin and on 28 April 1945 he was taken prisoner by the Russians during the fighting around the Hotel Excelsior. After many years suffering the rigours of gulag labour camps he returned to Spain in April 1954. His act of 'disobedience' in enlisting in the Waffen SS prevented him from joining the Spanish Army. He worked in the Bank of Spain's head office in Cordoba and died in that same city on 16 December 1981.

He appears here in the uniform of an *SS-Obersturmführer* (first lieutenant) in April 1945, in Berlin. On his M-44 camouflage uniform of the *Waffen SS* we can see his rank badges, a Spanish shield, and a Falangist badge. He is carrying the MP 40 submachine gun with which he was captured.

Left. Memoires of Alférez Ocañas, published on his return from Soviet concentration camps.

Right. Soviet soldiers during their advance on Germany; spring 1945.

Unteroffizier José Garayoa Murugarren, Armourer, 1st Blue Squadron; August 1941.

Oberleutnant Andrés Robles Cebrián, Pilot, 2nd Blue Squadron; September 1942.

Comandante Ángel Sálas Larrazábal, Pilot, Air Attaché in Berlin; 1943.

BLUE SQUADRON

Andrés Robles Cebrián was born in Palencia on 12 November 1917. On 20 September 1936, while in his second year of medicine, he volunteered for the Palencia Falangist militia. He fought on the Madrid Front with the 2nd Falangist *Bandera* of Palencia, where he received a serious back wound on 16 November of that same year. Once recovered he returned to the fray and in March 1937, he entered the *El Copero* Flying School just south of Sevilla. He initially flew with the 1-G-2 Fighter Group, Levante Air region, and later, from 20 November, with the 2-G-3 Fighter Group (1st Squadron), part of the Central Air Region. He saw out the war in Fighter Group 3-G-3. Among other important actions, in August of that year he shot down a Polikarpov I-16 *Rata* over the River Zújar/Cabeza de Buey sector (Extremadura Front). In Russia he served in the 2nd Blue Squadron (1st Flight). On 1 July 1942, when attempting to repel a Soviet attack on the airfield at Orel, his Me 109 F2 was damaged. The same day Robles witnessed the death of his fellow pilot, Flight Lieutenant Noriega, shot down by Russian fighters.

On his return to Spain he remained in the air force, retiring with the rank of air marshal. He died in Madrid on March 21, 2013.

Centre. Robles Cebrián during his time on the Russian Front, serving in the 2nd Blue Squadron. *(Robles family archive)*

Left. Several members of the 2nd Blue Squadron. On the right, side on, is Robles Cebrián. *(Robles family archive)*

Below. A photo of Robles Cebrián shortly before his death, during a conversation with the authors.

Robles during his time with the El Copero Fighter School *(Sevilla) (Canario Azaola archive)*

He is portrayed here as a Luftwaffe pilot wearing the summer flight uniform, on which we can see the emblem of the *Morato* Squadron.

José Garayoa Murugarren, born in Santa Clara (Navarra) on 28 December 1917, joined the *Tercio de Requetés Santiago* in August 1936. He took part in the *Tercio's* combat operations in the mountains north of Madrid (Navafría and Somosierra sector, among others) until January 1938, when he was sent to train as a specialist aircraft armourer in Tetuan. At the end of the course he joined the *Morato* Fighter Group (3-G-3) as a corporal armourer, remaining in that unit until the end of the Civil War. He served in the Russian campaign as an armourer with the rank of *unteroffizier* (sergeant) in the 1st and 2nd Blue Squadrons and, due to his experience with German aircraft, he was also attached for some time to the 3rd Blue Squadron. On his return to Spain he remained in the air force, retiring with the rank of squadron leader. He died in Madrid on 28 August 1995.

Sergeant armourer Garayoa is sketched on page 78 at the moment of pledging loyalty to the *Führer* in the fight against Communism in the *Luftwaffe* manner, along with the rest of the 1st Blue Squadron, on the apron of Werneuchen Airfield (Berlin) on the morning of 16 August 1941.

Ángel **Salas Larrazábal** was born in Orduña (Vizcaya) on 1 October 1906. He was an African war veteran who fought

Centre. An unofficial badge denoting the presence of Spanish airmen on the Russian Front. *(Santiago Guillén García collection)*

Left. Garayoa (in the centre) was in Russia for nearly two years, where he cut his teeth as an armourer. *(Santiago Guillén García archive)*

Right. Tunic of a Luftwaffe *Unteroffizier* with a Spanish badge on the sleeve. *(González Beroiz collection)*

Left. In the cockpit of his Messerschmitt Me 109, *Comandante* Salas shakes the hand of *Capitán* Arístides García López-Rengel, another 1st Blue Squadron ace, lost over the Russian Front on 27 November 1941.

Centre.. A nice close-up of Angel Salas wearing his German Luftwaffe uniform with an Individual Military Medal over his breast pocket.

for a number of months in a battery of the 11th Light Artillery Regiment (Burgos) but later switched to flying. He became a fighter ace during the Civil War, by the end of which he was commander of the 2-G-3 *Morato* Fighter Group. He flew 618 sorties, totalling 1,215 flying hours in which he scored seventeen victories and was shot down four times. In the skies over Russia he commanded the 1st Blue Squadron where he flew seventy sorties, scoring six victories and destroying two aircraft on the ground (he was shot down just once). He was promoted to the rank of honorary air marshal and died in Madrid on July 19, 1994.

He is seen on page 78 wearing the regulation air force uniform after 1943 and is sporting his most important decorations: the Individual Military Medal (with two barrettes, Civil War and Russia), Iron Cross 1st Class and, on his sleeve, the Collective Military Medal patch with two bars awarded for his service in the *Morato* Group in the Civil War.

Left. Salas waves before taking off in his Messerschmitt Bf 109.

Below. Event at the Spanish Embassy in Berlin. Standing next to the Ambassador, the Count of Mayalde, is, on his right, the Luftwaffe Major Angel Salas Larrazábal, Commander of the 1st Blue Squadron, and other Spanish officers of the Blue Division, together with a number of members of the Spanish legation in the German capital, including Celia Jiménez.

Above. Gloves, flying jacket, and winter flight equipment used by the Blue Squadron on the Russian Front. *(Santiago Guillén collection)*

Below. Colonel's cap, badges, ID card and insignia of the Spanish Air Force belonging to Bernardo Meneses Orozco, a pilot who was credited with six victories in the skies over Russia while serving in the 3rd and 4the Squadrons. *(Santiago Guillén collection)*

Below left. A Soviet LaGG 3 shot down by *Hauptmann* José Ramón Gavilán Ponce de León of the 3rd Squadron. *(An artistic representation by Ramiro Bujeiro)*

Above and below. Luftwaffe flight log and some flying equipment used by the Spaniards of the Blue Squadrons. *(Santiago Guillén collection)*

Hauptmann Manuel Bengoechea Menchaca, Pilot, 2nd Blue Squadron; summer 1942.

Oberleutnant José Luis Álvarez-Sala Morís, Medic, 1st Blue Squadron; March 1942.

Andrés Oñate Matienzo, Mechanic, 3rd Blue Squadron; May 1943.

Leutnant Javier Mª Guibert Amor, Pilot, 4th Blue Squadron; July 1943.

Above. Various items of *Luftwaffe* and Spanish Air Force equipment used by the men of the Blue Squadron. *(Santiago Guillén García collection)*

Manuel Bengoechea Menchaca was born in Madrid on 15 December 1911. He had been studying at the General Military Academy when, shortly after the Second Republic was declared, the academy was shut down by the government, obliging him to move to the Artillery Academy in Segovia. There, in 1934, he took part in the suppression of the October Revolution with his battery of the 2nd Coastal Artillery Regiment. In June, 1936, while in Madrid on leave, he was wounded in a bomb attack on the Café Aquarium. Just as he was recovering from his injuries and about to return to El Ferrol, the Civil War broke out and he was imprisoned in the improvised prison of San Antón in the city of Madrid. In January 1937, he sought refuge in the Mexican Embassy and succeeded in reaching the Nationalist Zone via Marseilles. He fought with the 15th Light Artillery Regiment as a captain at the North, Teruel, and Catalonia Fronts, among others. In 1940 he trained as a pilot in Badajoz and transferred to the air force.

At the head of the 1st Flight of the 2nd Blue Squadron he was the unit's top ace with three enemy aircraft shot down over Russia. After repatriation on December 22, 1942 he continued his military career in the air force. He died in Madrid, on September 18, 1965 when director of training of the air force with the rank of air commodore.

Centre. Manuel Bengoechea, wearing a Spanish Air Force uniform, years after returning from Russia. *(SHYCEA)*

Below. General Ritter von Greim awards medals to a number of members of the Blue Squadron at the Orel Airfield. Among them is *Capitán* Manuel Bengoechea.

Teniente Médico José Luis Álvarez-Sala of the Blue Squadron on his return from the Russian Front. Note the Spanish Legion badge he is wearing on the sleeve of his *Luftwaffe* tunic. (*Álvarez-Sala family archive*)

Flying Officer Bengoechea appears here at the Orel airfield, wearing his Iron Cross 2nd Class awarded on July 7, 1942 (he would later receive the 1st Class distinction).

José Luis Álvarez-Sala Morís was born in Gijón (Asturias) on August 17, 1912. After graduating in Medicine he survived the siege of the Simancas barracks where he was serving as a medic at the start of the Civil War. He was arrested and sentenced to death but was pardoned and drafted into the Republican Army until the fall of Santander, when he switched sides again. He ended the war as a provisional medical officer. He served on the Russian campaign in the 1st Blue Squadron as a medical flying officer. He retired in 1976 after working at the Central Air Hospital. He died in Madrid on January 1, 2003.

While serving as a medical flying officer in the *Luftwaffe*, Álvarez-Sala is shown here on his return to Spain, with a KVK2 won on the Russian campaign and the badge of the *Tercio de Extranjeros* (Foreign Regiment) sewn onto his blue tunic, denoting that he had served in the 3rd *Bandera* of the Legion during the Civil War.

Above. From right to left, Alférez Guibert, with pipe, posing with another other two officers of the 3rd Squadron, *Teniente de Intendencia* Rafael Soler Rodero, in the middle, and *Teniente Piloto* Miguel Martínez Vara de Rey. (SHYCEA)

Below. Official German *Luftwaffe* eagle during the Second World War.

Javier Mª Guibert Amor was born in Pamplona (Navarra), on November 18, 1917. On July 19, 1936 he joined the *Requeté*, serving in the *Tercio de Roncesvalles* (later to be renamed *General Mola*) on the Northern Front. At the battle of Teruel, like so many combatants on either side, he fell victim to frostbite and, after a brief stay at the Getafe garrison performing security duties, towards the end of 1938 he was admitted to the Elementary Flying School at Tablada Airfield. The Civil War ended before he could fly any combat missions, but he later joined the 3rd Blue Squadron (3rd Flight) with the

Left. Ángel Sánchez Albaladejo, *Capitán Capellán* (chaplain) of the 3rd Squadron. The *Luftwaffe* was created in 1935 by Hermann Goering and had no chaplains on the staff. Nevertheless, Spanish priests served in the Blue Squadrons wearing *Luftwaffe* uniforms. In this photo the chaplain's tunic surprisingly has epaulettes, whereas the uniforms of *Wehrmacht* chaplains did not. *(Sánchez Albaladejo family archive)*

rank of pilot officer. He was involved in four aerial combats in that squadron, scoring one victory, but he added two more victories to his tally (on August 6 and 10, 1943) with the 4th Squadron. After being repatriated he reached the rank of group captain before retiring from military life, but he continued flying as a test pilot for the aircraft builder AISA. He died in Madrid on April 24, 1993.

Guibert is shown on page 84 wearing a peaked hat and pilot badges of both the *Luftwaffe* and the Spanish Air Force.

Andrés Oñate Matienzo was born in Colindres (Cantabria) on July 4, 1920.

Above and left. Oñate Matienzo, air force mechanic, before leaving for the Russian Front. *(Oñate Matienzo archive)*

He served in the Civil War as an infantry bugler in the 75th Battalion of the 28th *La Victoria* Regiment, switching to the air force at the end of the conflict. While serving in the 22nd Fighter Regiment at Tablada, Sevilla, he joined the 3rd Blue Squadron as a specialist mechanic. After the war he left the air force and became an executive at Telefónica in Bilbao, where his car was the target of an ETA attack. He died in Almodóvar del Campo (Ciudad Real) on September 19, 2011.

Oñate is portrayed on page 84 as a corporal mechanic at the French *Luftwaffe* base at Saint-Jean-d'Angély in October 1942.

Kapitan zur See Pedro Fernández Martín, Fernández Martín Commission; November 1942.

Feldwebel Francisco Regueiro Martínez, Fernández de la Puente Commission; spring 1943.

Gonzalo, Todt Organization; 1942.

NAVY AND TODT ORGANIZATION

P edro Fernández Martín was born in Jerez de la Frontera (Cadiz) on 3 October 1898. After fighting in the Civil War as a destroyer captain (his most noteworthy action was while in command of the destroyer *Velasco-Ceuta* when he prevented the Republican destroyer *José Luis Díez* from crossing the Strait of Gibraltar), in 1940 he was appointed Director of the School of Naval Engineers and shortly afterwards, commander of the school's fleet. In February of that same year he visited the German Naval Engineering School at Wesermünde and went on to serve in the German Navy from 13 November 1942 to 11 March 1943, with the rank of captain. He served on minesweepers and was second-in-command of a German destroyer in the Baltic Sea area. On 30 December 1943, on board the destroyer *Jorge Juan*, he helped rescue four German seamen shipwrecked near Cape Ortegal, aided by the destroyer of the same class *Sánchez Barcáiztegui*. For that action he was awarded the Order of the German Eagle 1st Class with Swords on 8 September 1944. Between 1945 and 1948 he was once again Director of the School of Naval Engineers and commander of the school's fleet.

Later, with the rank of commodore, he would command the Mediterranean Naval Division, the Cartagena Arsenal, and the Balearics Naval Base. He went on to hold the rank of vice-admiral and the post of Captain General of the El Ferrol Maritime Department. He died in the city of El Ferrol on 31 October 1962.

One of the very few photos showing a Spaniard wearing the uniform of the *Kriegsmarine.* He is *Kapitan zur See* Fernández Martín, commander of the first Spanish Navy Commission in Germany.

A German eagle adorns the bridge of a *Kriegsmarine* destroyer.

Bujeiro has sketched him as a *Kriegsmarine* captain visiting the Tiergarten in Berlin in November 1942 at the start of his mission in Germany.

Francisco Regueiro Martínez was born in Puentedeume (La Coruña) on 15 December 1907. He volunteered for the navy in March 1931 and fought in the Civil War on board the heavy cruiser *Canarias*, reaching the rank of corporal during the conflict. He was one of the NCOs who sailed with the Fernández de la Puente Commission, taking part in naval operations in the Gulf of Finland sector. With the rank of engineer sergeant second class he served on board the tender *Nettelbeck*, which was dedicated, among other duties, to minesweeping missions off the coast of Memel (now Klaipeda), in the Baltic. The eleven members of the Fernández de la Puente Commission earned the right to wear the German badge for minesweepers, sub-chasers and escort-vessel units on their uniforms. On his return to Spain in 1943, Regueiro stayed in the navy, serving on board various cruisers, destroyers, minesweepers and sub-chasers until he retired in July 1959. We have no information regarding the date of his decease.

Regueiro is seen on page 88 in the service uniform of an engineer petty officer of the German Navy.

Spanish *Feldwebel* Bienvenido Manrrubia (left) and Francisco Regueiro (right) chatting with a German *Oberfeldwebel* on board one of the minesweepers of 1.Räumflotille on 12 May 1943. *(Manrrubia family archive, via Hermenegildo Franco)*

A *Stahlhelm* (steel helmet) with the stencil of the Todt Organization.

Gonzalo ... was a law student when he became one of the thousands of Spaniards who joined the Todt Organization. He joined voluntarily, unlike many Republican exiles. He made no secret of his Falangist ideology and soon joined the Blue Division. On his return from the campaign he completed his law studies and went to work in a government ministry in Madrid. He died in Madrid.

He is depicted on page 88 wearing a Todt Organization uniform on an unspecified date.

(Out of respect for the wishes of his family this man is not identified by his real name.)

Left. The Spaniard Gonzalo, in one of the few photos evidencing the presence of Falangist volunteers in the ranks of the German Todt Organization.

Below. Tunic and cap belonging to a member of the Todt Organization.

Below. Various badges and equipment belonging to volunteers of the Todt Organization.

Oberleutnant José Pedro de Rojas Folgueira, Head of the Blue Division *Feldpost;* June 1942.

Teniente Indalecio Hernández Collantes, Chaplain of the III/263rd; June 1942.

Hauptmann Juan Palomino Fariñas, Workshop Company. 250th Transport Group; summer 1943.

SERVICES

José Pedro de Rojas Folgueira was born in Madrid on 7 March 1913. When the Civil War broke out he was a member of the *FE de las JONS*, working as a postal clerk in Allariz (Lugo). His contribution to the war effort was to organize the local Falange and later to serve as an ancillary worker in the National Army's mail service. Two days after his wedding he joined the Blue Division where he took charge of the unit's field postal service (*Feldpost*). He served in Russia until his repatriation in August 1942, when he entered the Ministry of Foreign Affairs to take charge of diplomatic courier services in various European countries during the rest of war. In peacetime he went back to the Spanish postal service where

José de Rojas Folgueira (left), head of the Blue Division's *Feldpost* (field mail service) at Novgorod in the spring of 1942. *(Rojas Folgueira family archive)*

became Head of the Philatelic Service and director of the Caja Postal de Ahorros bank. He died in Madrid on 1 February 1988.

De Rojas is depicted in the summer of 1942 wearing the uniform of civilian functionaries in the *Wehrmacht*. He was given the rank of acting lieutenant in order to command the Division's field postal service. Note the Spanish ribbon bar and the Falangist badge on his breast pocket.

On the far right of the photo, *Teniente* De Rojas poses with Spanish and German Blue Division services staff. (Rojas Folgueira family archive)

Right and centre. Juan Palomino Fariñas, head of the Workshop Company of the 250th Transport Group at the Leningrad Front. *(Palomino Fariñas family archive)*

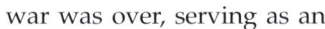

Juan Palomino Fariñas was born on 25 November 1913 in Madrid. On 18 July, the day of the uprising, he was studying law and serving as a provisional second lieutenant at the Montaña Barracks when it was besieged. When the barracks finally surrendered he miraculously survived the ensuing massacre. He was arrested and spent the rest of the war in the Madrid Model Prison, where he survived the *sacas*, whereby prisoners were taken out of their cells and summarily executed, until he was transferred to a psychiatric hospital after feigning madness. Some friendly fifth-column hand must have helped him since after the war he discovered that his file had mysteriously disappeared from the Directorate General for Security. He re-joined the army once the war was over, serving as an engineer. As captain in the Repairs Section of the 10th Engineers Regiment, he volunteered for the Russian Front on 26 June 1942, where he was stationed in the General HQ as head of the Workshop Company of the Transport Group. He was repatriated on 19 November 1943, after which he stayed in the army from which he retired with the rank of colonel. He died in Madrid on 8 September 1997.

Captain Palomino is shown on page 92 during a visit to the front line on the Leningrad Front during the summer of 1943. He is wearing an M-35 helmet with a Spanish decal and in the buttonhole of his M-36 tunic we can see the ribbon of the German KVK2 (awarded on 30 January 1943).

Alférez de Complemento Palomino with his hands up in surrender (first on the left) leaving the Montaña Barracks on Monday 20 July 1936. He miraculously escaped being executed by firing squad, the fate of most of his fellow soldiers.

Pablo Sagarra - Óscar González - Lucas Molina

In the centre, Padre Indalecio, next to Salvador López de la Torre (left) and soldier José María Gutiérrez del Castillo, at Grigorovo in the summer of 1942. *(FDA archive)*

Indalecio Hernández Collantes, born in Bolaños de Campos (Valladolid) on 30 January 1898, was ordained as a minister on 21 May 1921. He was called-up and served in the African war as a chaplain and when the Civil War broke out he volunteered for the 1st *Bandera Falange de León*, serving as chaplain at the Madrid Front. He also helped organize the Spanish youth organization of the time. In the Blue Division he served as chaplain to the 3rd Battalion of the 263rd in the first contingent, in which unit he was awarded the Iron Cross 2nd Class. After repatriation he worked as a priest at San Carlos Hospital in Madrid and was national chaplain for the *Frente de Juventudes* youth organization for a decade until his death in Madrid on 9 July 1960.

Father Indalecio's uniform has no epaulettes, as was the norm for a chaplain in the *Wehrmacht*, but he wears his lieutenant rank badges in the Spanish manner. As the staunch Falangist that he was, he wears a blue shirt under his tunic.

Left. Photograph of Father Indalecio, recently ordained in May of 1921.

Below. Medals and memorabilia of the chaplain of the Blue Division and Blue Legion, Heraclio Delgado Esteban.

Nurse Mercedes Gascón Sáinz, Königsberg Hospital; November 1943.

Hauptmann Antonio Ocaña Müller, 6th Company, 269th Infantry Regiment, Königsberg Hospital; February 1943.

Hauptmann Luis Arregui Gil, Riga Military Hospital Pharmacy; March 1944.

Above. Medals belonging to Capitán Arregui. *(Arregui family archive)*

Left. *Capitán de Farmacia* Luis Arregui Gil. He served in the campaign between August 1943 and April 1944. (Arregui family archive)

Luis Arregui Gil was born in Fustiñana (Navarra) on 10 February 1914. He had just completed his degree in pharmacy when the Civil War broke, so on 19 July he enlisted in Zaragoza as a volunteer. He joined a *bandera* of the Aragonese Falange although he was soon pulled off the front line when his commanding officer discovered that he was a pharmacist. From then until the end of the war he served in hospitals in the rear. While working in the pharmacy of the Pamplona Military Hospital, he joined the Blue Division with the 26th Marching Battalion. On arrival at the Russian Front he was sent to the hospital at Vilna and from there, now in the Blue Legion, to the hospital at Riga. He was sent back to Spain on 28 April 1944, where he worked at the Pamplona Military Hospital until he retired from the army. He died in the early hours of 18 July 1993, when he was awaiting his turn to take part in the Nocturnal Adoration of the Blessed Sacrament at his parish church in Pamplona.

Arregui is shown in the garden of the hospital at Riga in March 1944. He is wearing the insignia and patches corresponding to his rank of *Wehrmacht* pharmacy captain. The collar patch was similar to that worn by civilian functionaries, such as postal workers, although he was a military pharmacist in Spain.

Arregui Gil during the Civil War in which he served as a lieutenant pharmacist. *(Arregui family archive)*

Left. The first nurse on the left is Mercedes Gascón Sáinz. Koenigsberg, September 1943.

Below. Mercedes during a conversation with the authors in February of 2010.

Mercedes Gascón Sáinz was born in Zaragoza on 17 September 1914. The outbreak of the Civil War found her in San Sebastián. Once the city was liberated, she served as a nurse at a number of front line and rearguard hospitals. She joined the Lady Nursing Assistants Military Health Corps and left for Germany on 11 August 1943. It so happened that her husband, Julio Ruiz, who she married in 1937, was also serving with the Blue Division as a medic. Mercedes worked in Königsberg until the hospital shut down. Then late in April 1944, she returned to Spain with a group of sick and wounded volunteers. She left the army, lived in America for some time, and died in Madrid on 22 June 2010.

We see her on page 96 at the Königsberg hospital in the autumn of 1943. She is wearing an armband of the German Red Cross and a Spanish badge, but there are no arrows and yoke since she never belonged to the Falange.

Right. Mannequin of a Blue Division nurse. (FDA Museum)

Below left. Mercedes Gascón Sáinz.

Below right. Medals and other personal effects belonging to nurse Gascón.

Oberleutnant Ocaña Müller with two Spanish officers of the same rank, photographed at Hof an der Saale (Baviera) in January 1942, having recently joined the Division. *(Ocaña Müller family)*

Antonio Ocaña Müller, born in Ksar el-Kebir (Morocco) on 4 March 1916, joined the uprising in Granada where he was studying medicine. He served with the local militia known as the Spanish Volunteer Patriots who manned the city's defensive ring but he also fought in the Alcalá la Real (Jaén) sector. As a provisional second lieutenant he served in the 5th Lepanto Infantry Regiment and in the 1st Blue Arrows Mixed Brigade. By the end of the war he was a provisional lieutenant in the 31st Burgos Infantry Regiment. After attending an *Academia de Transformación* (an academy which trained provisional rank officers to qualify them for a substantive rank) he joined the Blue Division in January 1942 with the rank of lieutenant. He served in the 1st Company of the Anti-Tank Group until 19 March 1942, when he transferred to the 2nd Battalion of the 269th where he commanded either a section or a company (the 7th of the aforementioned battalion) until he was promoted to captain and given command of the 6th Company (June 1942). He was sent to the rear to recover from a knee injury sustained during the fighting at the Volkhov Pocket.

After returning to his 6th Company, he fought at the Battle of Poselok on 23 January 1943, where he was wounded three times on the same day. He was evacuated and then sent back to Spain to continue his convalescence there. He underwent thirteen operations until April 1945 when he was classified as 50 per cent disabled but fit for active service. He retired with the rank of colonel in 1981, although shortly afterwards he was promoted to honorary general. He died in Valladolid on 27 August 1995.

Ocaña is depicted at Königsberg Hospital in February 1943, where he was being treated for a major injury to the lower jaw caused by an explosive round. He is wearing the ribbons of the First Winter Medal and the KVK2, together with the black wound badge.

Centre. The then *Teniente Coronel* Ocaña Müller (right) with a Spanish uniform of the 1960s, wearing his German and Spanish medals, after a military ceremony of the IPS military academy at Monte La Reina (Zamora) *(Ocaña Müller family)*

Left. Passport issued on 17 January 1942 by the Military Government of Granada for *Teniente* Ocaña's safe passage to Irún to join the Blue Division. *(Ocaña Müller family)*

Joaquín Jiménez de Anta was born in Arévalo (Ávila), on 8 March 1908. In 1927 he served as quartermaster lieutenant in the final throes of the African War. The rebellion on 18 July 1936 found him attached to the Sub-Secretariat of the Ministry of War (Quartermaster Office). He decided to stay in the Republican Army working as an undercover agent. His adventures during the war are the stuff of a Hollywood action movie. He was arrested as a spy and taken to the provisional prison at Atocha, Madrid, although he would later be released through lack of evidence. He continued to operate as a fifth columnist as part of the Antonio Network, whose leader, Quartermaster Lieutenant Antonio Rodríguez Aguado, would later face a firing squad. He joined the Spanish Communist Party to provide himself with better cover, before taking refuge in the Turkish Embassy. When the members of the SIM (Military Information Service) stormed the embassy, he was once again arrested and imprisoned in Barcelona in Montjuic Castle. His luck continued to hold as he managed to escape being killed in the mass execution of prisoners at El Collell during the Republican withdrawal in February 1939. Joaquín served in the Blue Division between March 1942 and August 1943. After being promoted to major he was given command of the Supply Company of the Quartermaster Group. On his return to Spain he completed his degree in medicine and in 1953 left the army with the rank of major to pursue a career as a gynaecologist. He died in Barcelona on 25 June 1975.

He is shown here protecting himself from the rain at Mestelevo in May 1943, with an overcoat bearing the appropriate rank and specialty badges.

Centre. Jiménez de Anta, with visor cap, commander of the Supply Company of the 250th Quartermaster Group. Mestelevo, on the Leningrad Front. June 1943. *(Jiménez de Anta family archive)*

Left. On the left, Jiménez de Anta before his promotion to *Comandante*. On the right, half cut-off by the photographer, we see *Capitán de Intendencia* Sebastián Moll Carbó. *(Jiménez de Anta family archive)*

Right. Wehrmacht collar patches and insignia belonging to veterinary officer Miguel Martín Ortiz *(Martín Ortiz family collection)*

Centre. Teniente José María Hidalgo Chapado, a vet like Martín Ortiz, was responsible for the veterinary service of the 1st Artillery Group in the first Blue Division contingent *(Hidalgo Chapado family archive)*

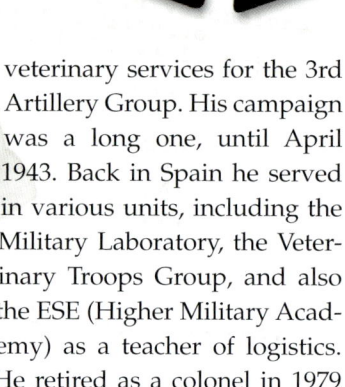

Miguel Martín Ortiz was born in Villafranca de Córdoba (Cordoba) on 8 February 1915. He joined the *FE de las JONS* in 1935, and on 19 July 1936 he volunteered for the 1st Heavy Artillery Regiment in Cordoba. Later he served in a Falangist militia unit supporting the telephone services of various columns on the Andalusian front. On graduating as a vet, he was promoted to veterinary officer, 3rd class, and sent to the Écija Horse Rearing and Training Depot. From there he transferred to the 31st Division and before the end of the war he moved again, this time to the 122nd Division. After attending the Military Health Academy, he joined the Military Veterinary Corps. In July 1941 he joined the Blue Division in which he was in charge of

veterinary services for the 3rd Artillery Group. His campaign was a long one, until April 1943. Back in Spain he served in various units, including the Military Laboratory, the Veterinary Troops Group, and also the ESE (Higher Military Academy) as a teacher of logistics. He retired as a colonel in 1979 and died in Madrid on 11 December 1984.

Martín Ortiz is shown on page 100 driving a sled at Novgorod in December 1941. His epaulettes bear the insignia of a veterinary captain.

Above. Teniente Coronel Miguel Martín Ortiz, with his Blue Division badge shakes the hand of the Head of State, Francisco Franco *(Martín Ortiz family archive)*

Left. Comandante Sarmiento Ramos, head of the Blue Division veterinary services, looking at a sample through a microscope *(family archive Sarmiento Ramos)*

Capitán Ripoll (fellow officer and friend of Maximiliano Amaro) shortly before his repatriation to Spain. He was head of quartermaster services of the Blue Division. *(Ripoll family archive, via Retógenes Association)*

Maximiliano Amaro Lasheras was born in La Línea de la Conception (Cadiz), on 10 August 1917. While studying law, he joined the first incarnation of the SEU, and during the Civil War he served in a Falangist *Centuria*, taking part in the conquest of a number of Andalusian towns, including Estepona and Marbella. After qualifying as a provisional second lieutenant, he fought with the 3rd *Tabor* of the 4th *Larache* Regular Forces Group, always in Andalusia and Extremadura. By the end of the war he was a provisional lieutenant. After graduating in law, he joined the Military Intervention Corps and in June 1942 he volunteered for the Russian front where he asked to be assigned to a combat unit, the 3rd Company of the Sappers Battalion. He fought in the Battle of Krasny-Bor, during which he was wounded while trying to halt the advance of Soviet tanks. Repatriated in May 1943, he remained in the army until retiring with the rank of colonel. He died in Madrid on 23 October 2005.

Amaro Lasheras on page 100 in 1945 as a captain (he was promoted while in Russia) wearing a Spanish uniform. He is wearing decorations awarded during his two campaigns, including a Medal of Suffering for the Motherland, Iron Cross 2nd Class, Infantry Assault badge, *Cruz de Guerra* (War Cross) and a Wound Badge.

Below. A lunch in honour of Capitán Amaro on his return from Russia. On his Spanish uniform he wears his Iron Cross 2nd Class in the German manner, on the third button hole of his tunic. Among those present were Camilo José Cela (second row, second from the right) *(Amaro family archive, via Retógenes Association)*

Above. On the way to the Russian Front. On the far left, Maximiliano Amaro stands next to a number of fellow Spaniards and a German. *(Amaro family archive, via Retógenes Association)*

Below. Red Cross with two bars, Medal of Suffering for the Motherland with one bar, 1936-1939 Campaign Medal, and Spanish Division of Volunteers in Russia Campaign Medal, all belonging to Amaro. *(Amaro family collection, via Retógenes Association)*

Teniente Coronel (Artillery, General Staff) Ignacio Moyano Araiztegui, Assistant Military Attaché in Berlin; July 1943.

José Mª Finat de la Blanca y Escrivá de Romaní, Spanish Ambassador in Berlin; September 1942.

Celia Jiménez Costeira, *Madrina* (godmother) of the Blue Division; May 1943.

DIPLOMATS

José Mª Finat de la Blanca y Escrivá de Romaní (Count of Mayalde) was born in Madrid on 11 February 1904. Despite his Falangist leanings (he was a personal friend of José Antonio), in February 1936 he ran for election in the province of Toledo as a candidate of CEDA (Spanish Confederation of Autonomous Right-wing Groups). In the Civil War he fought as a provisional artillery officer, earning an Individual Military Medal at the Moncloa Campus, Madrid on 14 April 1937, although he had already distinguished himself at Villaviciosa de Odón the previous November when his artillery piece destroyed four tanks. During the first period of the Blue Division he was Spanish Ambassador to Germany (1940 to 1942), his removal from that post being due to the forced resignation of his patron, Foreign Secretary Serrano Suñer. The count also held a number of other important positions, including Director General of Security, Civil Governor of the province of Madrid, Mayor of Madrid, and Member of Parliament under Franco. After retiring from political life, he became a leading figure in the world of bullfighting as owner of the

Count of Mayalde, artilleryman and Falangist in the Civil War, a campaign in which he was awarded the Individual Military Medal.

Conde de Mayalde breed of fighting bulls. He died in Madrid on 9 June 1995.

He is shown here in Berlin as Ambassador in the autumn of 1941. On his uniform we can see his Civil War decorations and the shield of the Falange's Foreign Service on his right breast pocket.

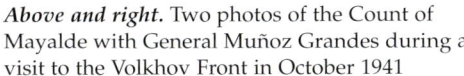

Above and right. Two photos of the Count of Mayalde with General Muñoz Grandes during a visit to the Volkhov Front in October 1941

Left. Celia Jiménez, the *madrina* (godmother) of the Blue Division, in Berlin in conversation with a number of Blue Division officers, among whom standing next to her, is *Capitán* José Martín Álvarez Chas de Berbén (*Álvarez Chas de Berbén family archive*)

Centre. Celia visiting the Russian Front *(FDA archive)*

Celia Jiménez Costeira was the widow of Captain Rafael Jiménez Benhamou, a pilot who was killed in combat on 10 December 1936. After working as a nurse in various Spanish military hospitals, she went to Berlin where Pilar Primo de Rivera, sister of the founder of the Falangist Movement, gave her the job of leading the Women's Section of the Falange's Foreign Service in Germany. Celia became the *madrina* (godmother) *par excellence* of the Blue Division; her Spanish language programme dedicated to the soldiers of the Blue Division broadcast on Radio Berlin was legendary. Over 500 letters would arrive at her studio every day, which she would read and sort one by one. She had three daily broadcasts; the first, just after noon (thirty minutes), the second in the early evening (twenty minutes), and there was also one at night to help send the Spanish soldiers off to sleep. After returning from Germany she became Chief Steward for the airline AVIACO. She lived out her last years in Santa Cruz de Tenerife and she is buried there in the Santa Lastenia cemetery.

She is seen on page 104 saluting in her Falangist Movement uniform during an official act in Berlin.

Celia at Grafenwöhr with Muñoz Grandes and other Blue Division commanders and *FET y de los JONS* staff.

Right. Visiting the Blue Division wounded. Moyano, in his Spanish uniform, is helping with the distribution of gifts to Spanish hospital patients.

Centre. This photograph was taken on 18 July 1943, at Pokrovskaya on the Russian Front. *Teniente Coronel* Moyano with *Comandante* García Andino. Behind walks the German Chief of Liaison Staff, *Oberst* Knüppel. *(Ripoll family archive, via Retógenes Association)*

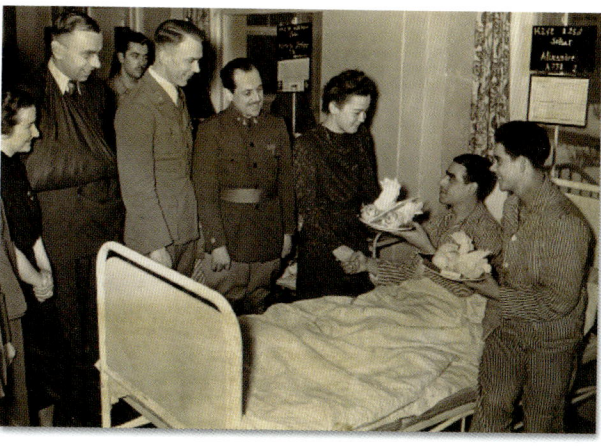

Ignacio Moyano Araiztegui (Marqués de Inicio) was a hero of the African War. On 20 August 1925, he won the Laureate Cross of Saint Ferdinand in an artillery duel as a lieutenant commanding the batteries on the Island of Alhucemas against enemy positions at Yebel-Sedum. In 1932, he married Blanca Doussinague (from a diplomatic family). In June 1941, he joined the Blue Division but a bicycle accident in Grafenwöhr left him with a broken collar bone, which prevented him from taking part in the campaign. He was sent home, but on 28 November 1941, he took up a post at the Berlin Embassy as an assistant military attaché, which brought him into contact with Blue Division commanders and occasionally required him to visit the Russian front. After the fall of Germany, he stayed in the army. His last posting was as colonel of the 71st Artillery Regiment. He died in Madrid on 5 November 1955 holding the rank of brigadier general.

In the illustration, Moyano is seen at the Leningrad Front on 18 July 1943, celebrating his recent promotion to lieutenant colonel at the Blue Division General HQ at the Pokrovskaya czarist mansion. On his Spanish uniform we see his insignia and sash of the General Staff Corps (belonging to the 33rd promotion of April 1936), together with the Laureate Cross of Saint Ferdinand and, naturally, the Cross of the Order of the German Eagle with Swords, at his throat.

A German general is awarded a number of Spanish medals on July 18, 1943. On the left of the photo, the then Assistant Military Attaché at the Spanish Embassy in Berlin, *Teniente Coronel* Ignacio Moyano Araiztegui.

Coronel Ricardo Villalba Rubio, 5th Alhucemas Regular Forces Group; Melilla 1951.

Coronel Florencio de Apellániz Fernández, Director of the Armed Police Academ;1975.

Comandante Prudencio Ortega Gil, Military Household of the Caliph of Tetuán; 1949.

POST-WAR

Thousands of volunteers were either soldiers before leaving for Russia or became soldiers afterwards. As we have seen in previous illustrations, on returning to Spain many of them continued to proclaim their allegiance to the Blue Division and its spirit on their post-war uniforms.

Florencio de Apellániz Fernández, born in Coca (Segovia) on 29 September 1916, joined the Blue Division as a student on 30 July 1936 in a *Centuria* of the Falange in Valladolid. He fought as an officer in the *San Quintín* Regiment and in the Legion (12th and 16th *Banderas*). He enlisted in the Blue Division as a lieutenant and after being promoted to captain he commanded the 4th Company of the 262nd and the 2nd Company of the Mobile Reserve Battalion of the 250th, before being repatriated in July 1943. He took part in the Ifni-Sahara War from November 1957, as commander-in-chief of the 2nd *Bandera* of the *Tercio Gran Capitán 1º de la Legión*. During the fighting he took command of an *ad hoc* group of units. After the war he remained in the army until he died on 22 November 1980 in Madrid, shortly after retiring as a colonel.

A line-up of legionnaires. Apellániz served with the Spanish Legion in the Spanish Civil War and the Ifni-Sahara War in 1958, commanding a combat group

A magnificent portrait of the then *Teniente Provisional de Infantería* Florencio de Apellániz Fernández, when he was a student at the Infantry Military Academy after the Spanish Civil War had ended. On his left sleeve he is sporting to two wound chevrons and a Collective Military Medal. Over his left breast pocket, we can see the badge showing he is a *Teniente Provisional* (two stars above a black rectangle), and a Medal of Suffering for the Motherland. *(Apellániz family archive)*

Coronel Apellániz, director of the Armed Police Academy, addressing the new intake. *(Apellániz family archive)*

Florencio is shown here as colonel director of the Special Armed Police Academy in 1975. On his slate-grey uniform we can see two wound chevrons (Teruel 5 February 1938, and Ebro 28 July 1938), a Collective Military Medal, the Legion veteran badge (with bars for fourteen years' service), together with his KVK2 and Iron Cross 2nd Class which he earned in Russia.

Ricardo Villalba Rubio was born in Toledo on 24 January 1892. At the age of fourteen he began his military career in the infantry. He served in Africa (11th San Fernando Regiment and Indigenous Police) and in the Civil War, where fought with distinction in the defence of the Toledo Alcázar in the Soria Division (Moscardó) – he was wounded three times and recommended for an individual Laureate Cross – and as commander of the 1st Brigade of the 74th Division. In the Russian campaign he commanded the 263rd Regiment between July 1942 and February 1943, then with the rank of colonel, earning an Iron Cross 2nd Class.

Above. In Russia, Villalba commanded the 263rd Infantry Regiment between July 1942 and February 1943. *(Villalba family archive)*

Left. Ricardo Villalba wearing his brigadier's dress uniform. Among the most important of his many medals were those won during the Russian campaign. *(Villalba family archive)*

He held various positions in the army and in civilian life: Deputy Mayor for Madrid, Nacional Inspector of Physical Education and Sport, and Vice-President of the International Federation of Physical Education. He retired as an honorary major general and died in Madrid on 10 May 1994.

Right. Villalba, in civvies, at an event commemorating the Blue Division in the 1960s in Madrid in front of the *Cuartel Inmemorial del Rey* (the headquarters of the King's Immemorial Infantry Regiment). Sitting beside him is Ramón Serrano Súñer, the creator of the Blue Division. *(Villalba family archive)*

Centre. Photo in Russia of the then *Comandante* Prudencio Ortega Gil, commander of the 250th Anti-Tank Group of the Blue Division. Far Right. Order of the Medahuia. *(Ortega family archive and collection)*

In Ramiro Bujeiro's illustration he is shown as a colonel of the 5th *Alhucemas* Regular Forces Group in Melilla, in the year 1951.

Prudencio Ortega Gil was born in Fuentepinilla (Soria) on 13 May 1908. A second lieutenant in 1926, the following year he fought in the Africa campaign for a few months in the *Alcántara* Light Cavalry Regiment in the 14th Cavalry Division. He served in the Protectorate in various cavalry units and by the start of the Civil War he was a lieutenant in the 3rd *Mehal-la Jalifiana* at Larache. By the end of the conflict he had been promoted to captain and it was with this rank that he joined the Blue Division in June 1942. He commanded the 1st Squadron of the Reconnaissance Group during the fighting on the Volkhov and at Leningrad and, after a further promotion to major he led the Anti-Tank Group from 23 March 1943 to September of that same year, when he was sent home. He remained in the army until retiring with the rank of cavalry brigadier. He died in Madrid on 2 September 1970.

He is shown on page 108 in 1949 when he was head of the military household of His Highness the Caliph of Tetuan. On the right-hand side of his uniform as commander of the *Meha-la Jalifiana* he wears the Order of Mehdauia (*Saada* class), the lanyard of an officer attached to the military household of the 2nd Caliph (of Tetuan), and the *Mehal-la* badge with four red service bars. On the left-hand side, among other decorations, he wears several red Military Merit Crosses, two War Crosses, 2nd and 1st Class Iron Crosses, the KVK2 and the General Infantry Assault Badge.

Another photo of Ortega at the front. On his arrival in Russia he was posted to the 250th Exploration Group. *(Ortega family archive)*

Capitán José Martín Álvarez Chas de Berbén, Colonial Guard, Bata (Spanish Guinea) 1946.

Teniente Rafael Martínez Aguilar, 3rd Saguia-El Hamra Nomad Group; December 1957.

Sargento Vicente García Mercé, Spanish Legion; November 1945.

PABLO SAGARRA - ÓSCAR GONZÁLEZ - LUCAS MOLINA

Left. Wearing the uniform of the Colonial Guard, *Capitán* Chas de Berben reviews his troops at Bata, the largest city of what was then Spanish Guinea. *(Chas de Berbén family archive)*

Right. Array of medals belonging to *Comandante* Chas de Berben, won in Spain and in Russia. *(Chas de Berbén family collection)*

José Martín Álvarez Chas de Berbén was born in Pontevedra on 24 August 1917. He joined the Segovia *Requeté* (*Tercio San Rafael*), operating in the Guadarrama area until 15 August 1936, when he transferred to the *Tercio del Rey*. As a provisional second lieutenant he served in the 10th Battalion of the 28th La Victoria Infantry Regiment and in the 5th *Tabor* of the 3rd Ceuta Regular Forces Group. He fought at Brunete, where he was wounded, and at the breach of the Castellón Front, where he was also injured (19 February 1938).

With the substantive rank of captain he left for Russia in June 1942 to take command of the 5th Company of the 263rd Regiment. He was twice wounded; on 26 July at the Volkhov Pocket and on 24 October at Pushkin, this latter time by shrapnel from a hand grenade. Once recovered, he returned to the front until on 24 September he received yet another wound, while defending the *El Alcázar* position. After returning to Spain on 3 January 1944, he continued his convalescence at the Gómez Ulla Hospital in Madrid. He went on to serve in Guinea and Ifni, among other postings. On 11 August 1957, while serving at Ifni as commander of the 1st Police Group, José Martín met his death; the aircraft he was flying in plunged into the Atlantic, killing him and all the crew.

In the sketch the commander of the 2nd Company of the Colonial Guard at Bata (Equatorial Guinea) is protecting his head with a pith helmet and wearing the dress uniform for colonial officers. He has no fewer than eight wound chevrons, the

Centre and left. Two photos of the heroic *Capitán* José Martín Álvarez Chas de Berbén during his time with the Blue Division. In Paris, on his way back to Spain, he fell in love with a young Spanish-German woman, Mercedes Lenze López, whom he would later marry. Her brother, José Carlos, was also a volunteer in the Blue Division; his photo can be seen on the front cover of this book, sporting a War Merit Cross *(Kriegsverdienstkreuz)* 2nd Class with Swords. *(Chas de Berbén family archive)*

Hitler's Spanish Division

Left. Rafael Martínez Aguilar's dog tag. *(family collection Martínez Aguilar)*

Right. Martínez Aguilar, standing between two fellow soldiers at the Leningrad Front. *(Martínez Aguilar family archive)*

Collective Military Medal (won at Alto de los Leones), the Iron Cross 1st Class, and silver infantry assault and wound badges.

Rafael Martínez Aguilar was born in Cabezas de San Juan (Sevilla), on 6 February 1923. He was a teenager living in Medina Sidonia (Cadiz) during the Civil War but volunteered for the Blue Division in March 1942 while serving with the 24th Artillery Regiment at Jerez. He served in the regimental Staff of the 250th Artillery in charge of radio equipment of the signals service where he was promoted to corporal and recommended for promotion to sergeant. Among other decorations he was awarded two red Military Merit Crosses and a KVK2. He was repatriated in December 1943 where he remained in the army until 1961, when he joined the Madrid Local Police force after sitting an open competitive exam. He retired in 1977 as a police inspector and head of traffic. He died in October 2015 in Madrid.

He is shown on page 112 during the Ifni War, as lieutenant in the Headquarter Company of the 3rd Saguia-El Hamra Nomad Group, in December 1957.

Right. Rafael Martínez Aguilar strolling through the gardens surrounding the Pavlovsk Palace, occupied at the time by the Headquarter Company of the 250th Artillery Regiment. *(Martínez Aguilar family archive)*

Below. Teniente Martínez Aguilar (to the left, wearing a white uniform) at the head of his section in Africa. *(Martínez Aguilar family archive)*

Right. Citation for the Commemorative Medal for Spanish Volunteers in the Struggle Against Bolshevism awarded to *Sargento* García Mercé of the 262nd Regiment. *(García Mercé family collection)*

Left. Four wound chevrons from *Sargento* Vicente García Mercé's uniform. *(García Mercé family collection)*

Vicente García Mercé was born in Bicorp (Valencia) on 29 May 1906. Orphaned at the age of twelve, he joined the Legion in July 1925. He served in the *Tercio Duque de Alba* (4th Company, 2nd *Bandera*), taking part in the fighting at Alhucemas and in the storming of Monte Palomar. He graduated in 1930, worked for a while in France, and re-enlisted in June 1936. He was wounded in the storming of Badajoz with the 16th Company of the 4th *Bandera*, and was wounded again in the Mainar sector (Zaragoza). He also fought at Teruel and on the Ebro. In July 1943, as a sergeant, he left to join the Russian campaign with the 6th Company of the 262nd Regiment. At the *El Dedo* position he fought with distinction and was wounded in the last great battle of the Blue Division, on 12 October 1943. Among other decorations, he received the *Cruz de Guerra*. In 1946 he retired from the army and went to work for the Badajoz urban transport company. He died in that same city on 2 September 1984.

On his 1945 uniform on page 112 we can see his four wound chevrons (three wounds in the Civil War and one in Russia), two Collective Laureate Crosses awarded to his *bandera* for its performance at the Moncloa Campus (10 May 1937) and during crossing of the Ebro at Quinto (3 August 1938), the Medal of Suffering for the Motherland, a wound badge, and several others.

Right. Collective Laureate with repetition bar and Collective Military badges belonging to the uniform of *Sargento* García Mercé. *(García Mercé family collection)*

Left. García Mercé, squatting on the right, hugging his dog 'Lolo', surrounded by a number of fellow soldiers of the 2nd *Tercio* of the Legion at Dar Riffien. *(García Mercé family archive)*